INDIA, Restructured

India is no longer a future option.
It is a present decision.

EU–India FTA

Rahul Hingmire, Advocate & Corporate Lawyer

notionpress.com

INDIA • SINGAPORE • MALAYSIA

ISBN
Paperback 979-8-90451-360-3
Hardcase 979-8-90479-534-4

India, Restructured—First Edition, 2025–26

About This Edition

The India–EU Free Trade Agreement, referenced throughout this book, was concluded in 2025 following negotiations spanning more than a decade. Its provisions are being brought into force in stages. Tariff schedules, services commitments, and regulatory cooperation mechanisms are being operationalised progressively by both parties as domestic legislative and administrative processes are completed.

This edition reflects the FTA framework and its key provisions as understood at the time of publication. The indicative tariff rates, the sector analysis and the compliance frameworks described throughout are based on the agreement as concluded and on applicable Indian law and regulatory practice as at 2025–26.

As the FTA's implementation milestones are reached, including the formal entry into force of specific tariff schedules, the operationalisation of services commitments, and the establishment of joint FTA administration bodies, a revised edition of this book will be published reflecting those developments. Readers engaged in active transaction planning are encouraged to verify current implementation status with their advisers.

Published by Notion Press

This book is dedicated to those who gave me roots strong enough to stand firm, and wings wide enough to take risks.

About the Author

Rahul Hingmire is an Advocate & Corporate Lawyer practising at the Bombay High Court and the Co-Founder and Co-Managing Partner of Vis Legis Law Practice, Advocates, a multi-office Indian law firm with offices in Mumbai, New Delhi, Pune, and Hyderabad.

He advises Indian and international businesses, investors, founders, and management teams on cross-border transactions, India entry structuring, foreign direct investment, mergers and acquisitions, insolvency and bankruptcy, arbitration, commercial contracts, and strategic legal advisory. His work combines legal precision with commercial understanding, especially in matters involving business expansion, restructuring, execution risk, and dispute exposure across sectors such as real estate, manufacturing, healthcare, hospitality, consumer business, and technology.

Over the years, Rahul has advised on domestic and cross-border acquisitions, private investments, joint ventures, and complex business arrangements, while also representing clients in litigation, arbitration and insolvency matters before key courts and tribunals in India. His practice reflects a strong focus on practical execution, board-level risk assessment and long-term business value.

Rahul is also the host of the podcast series 'Due Diligence with Rahul,' where he interviews leading legal voices from major Indian and multinational organisations. He is a regular speaker at 'Redevelopment Roundtable Discussions' and 'Founder-Investor Boardroom' Sessions across Mumbai, Pune, Thane, and Hyderabad, both pro bono knowledge initiatives of Vis Legis Law Practice, Advocates.

Rahul is an angel investor and mentor to legal tech, fintech, defence tech, and health tech startups and their founders across India. He serves in board and advisory roles with Earlyseed Ventures Pvt. Ltd. and Sterling Workforce Enterprises Pvt. Ltd. He is also the President of Bhagyouday Bahudeshiya Education Society, an educational institution established in 1989.

His views and analysis have appeared in leading publications and media platforms, including The Economic Times, Mint, Moneycontrol, Business Standard, Hindustan Times, Forbes, and CNBC-TV18. He was recognised among 'Business World Legal's 40 Under 40 (2025)' and received 'the Top Managing Partner Law Firm' Recognition by Fortune Group, India (2025). He is a regular speaker at business forums, international conventions, industry events, startup and investor platforms, MSME networks, and university forums in India and abroad. He is frequently invited to speak on legal strategy, transactions, disputes, governance, investments, cross-border business, real estate, and practical business decision-making.

He is the author of ***'54 Legal Secrets Before You Sign a Redevelopment Agreement.'***

INDIA, RESTRUCTURED is his second book.

Connect with **Rahul Hingmire, Advocate & Corporate Lawyer**

LinkedIn **Instagram**

Testimonials

It is a pleasure to recommend the latest book of Rahul, whose work on the EU–India Free Trade Agreement reflects not only exceptional legal expertise, but also a rare depth of understanding of today's global realities. Beyond his professionalism, what really impressed me about Rahul is his empathy and balanced judgment—qualities that are indispensable in navigating complex international frameworks. He represents the modern lawyer: sharp, adaptable, and fully aligned with the demands of an evolving world.

This book is a must-read for anyone seeking meaningful legal insight into the historic opportunity presented by the EU–India Free Trade Agreement.

Andreea Vlănțoiu

Managing Partner, Vlănțoiu și Asociații, Bucharest, Romania

A respected Romanian legal professional with strong expertise in data, AI, crypto, technology laws, and international legal advisory.

I have had the pleasure of knowing Rahul through our professional network and have followed his commercial work with interest. He is knowledgeable, responsive and clearly well regarded in the commercial legal space in India.

Andrew Robins

Partner, RSW Law Limited, London, United Kingdom

A seasoned UK legal professional bringing strong commercial insight and international legal perspective.

I have known Advocate Rahul Hingmire for several years as a leading lawyer, entrepreneur, and friend. In my experiences collaborating with him, I was impressed by his ability to distil complex legal concepts and share actionable takeaways in an easy-to-understand manner for both legal and business audiences. His insights on the India–EU Free Trade Agreement will open doors for well-structured businesses to make the most of it!

Arjun Bala

Managing Director & Patent Agent, Metayage, Bengaluru, India

An intellectual property professional with strong expertise in patents, innovation strategy, and technology-focused advisory.

Rahul is one of those rare professionals who speaks the language of business, not just law. He combines deep expertise with genuine clarity, always getting to the point and understanding the stakes. Interacting with him never felt like a legal consultation; it felt like a conversation with someone who truly wants you to walk away wiser.

This book will be a go-to for anyone serious about the India-EU opportunity, and I can't think of a better person to have written it.

Bronika Gandhi

Chief of Staff, Aeroflex Enterprises Ltd., Mumbai, India

A dynamic legal & business professional bringing strong leadership support, strategic coordination, and execution focus.

Rahul and his team have handled our real estate and corporate matters for several years with great skill and a strong solution-oriented approach. I'm sure this book will offer the same value and clarity that he consistently brings to the Brahm Group of Companies across the globe.

Bhavook Tripathi

Founder, Chairman & CEO, The Brahm Group of Companies

Canada, India, Spain, Mexico, USA & UAE

A global business leader and mentor with a strong vision for building enterprises across markets, sectors, and geographies

Rahul Hingmire brings a rare blend of legal precision and commercial insight, grounded in hands-on cross-border experience in his new book. As a lawyer engaged in international transactions myself, I found this book invaluable—it clearly sets out India's market entry, FDI structuring, contracts, compliance, dispute management, and exits, offering practical guidance for anyone considering business or investment in India. The book highlights a critical truth: the FTA creates opportunity, but only structured businesses can capture it.

Rahul's ability to turn policy into actionable strategy, combined with foresight and deep commitment, makes this work a testament to his expertise and vision of India as a platform for long-term growth.

Elsa Law

Founder and Partner, Elsa Law & Co. Solicitors, Hong Kong SAR

A senior Hong Kong lawyer with 25+ years of experience in commercial law, employment, litigation, family law, succession planning, probate, and cross-border advisory.

It is a privilege to work alongside such a forward-thinking and solution-driven colleague. He approaches even the most complex challenges with intellectual curiosity, precision, and a remarkable openness to innovative, sometimes unconventional, solutions—always grounded in solid legal reasoning. His strong technical expertise is matched by his exceptional ability to build and nurture meaningful professional relationships across our international alliance. He consistently demonstrates respect, empathy, and integrity, earning the trust and esteem of peers. In every respect, he embodies the highest standards of our profession and is a truly valued colleague and partner.

Enrica Maggi

CEO, Worldwide Independent Lawyers League (WILL), Klagenfurt am Wörthersee, Austria

A global legal community leader supporting independent lawyers through international networks, trust-based relationships, and cross-border professional opportunities.

Rahul is a highly competent lawyer with a strong command of global markets and a keen understanding of cross-sector dynamics. His ability to adapt swiftly to technological developments and integrate them into legal strategy sets him apart. In our interactions, I have found him to be both insightful and pragmatic, offering well-structured, business-oriented solutions. He combines deep legal expertise with a forward-thinking mindset, making him a trusted advisor in complex international matters.

Fatma Karakülah

Founder, Turkius Law, Istanbul, Türkiye & Cologne, Germany

A respected international legal professional bringing a strong cross-border perspective across Türkiye, Germany, and global business matters.

Rahul brings rare clarity to the complex world of cross-border business and regulation. His ability to translate policy into practical business strategy makes this work especially valuable for anyone looking to navigate the India–EU opportunity.

Ganeshprasad S.

Chief Operating Officer, Think School, Mumbai, India

A YouTube knowledge leader known for making complex geopolitical, business, and economic case studies simple, sharp, and highly engaging for India's digital-first audience.

As a Chartered Accountant specializing in business internationalization, I regard Adv. Rahul Hinghmire is a professional of the highest caliber, capable of combining legal rigor with operational vision, offering with this work an authoritative and indispensable reference for European companies seeking to structure and expand their presence in India.

Giuseppe Sagone

Partner, Studio Zanlungo, Milan, Italy

A respected finance professional contributing valuable international perspective and cross-border insight.

Rahul is an incredibly approachable and insightful professional who genuinely enjoys supporting and uplifting others. He brings a rare combination of curiosity, kindness, and warmth to every interaction, which makes working with him both productive and enjoyable.

I consulted Rahul in 2024 regarding the Indian market for an AI project I was working on, and he was able to guide me through complex technical and legal terminology with remarkable clarity and patience. His ability to explain nuanced concepts in a clear and understandable manner was extremely valuable. I highly appreciate his professionalism, expertise, and collaborative spirit.

Jelena Nad

Founder, Experiment 6, Mexico City, Mexico

A legal marketing professional with strong experience in law firm, tax, accounting, notary, and HR sector communication and positioning.

My professional journey to Mumbai in January 2026 gave me a profound masterclass in the synergy between international legal excellence and visionary business leadership. Engaging with Attorney Rahul Hingmire and his esteemed team offered a rare glimpse into a practice where meticulous legal structuring meets a deeply human and empowerment-driven approach. Attorney Rahul Hingmire embodies a rare combination: a formidable commercial mind that is sharp, strategic, and precise, along with the temperament of a true gentleman. His ability to facilitate cross-border dialogues and build meaningful international business relationships is exceptional. During our professional exchange, it became evident that his philosophy reflects the core message of this book: while frameworks like the India–EU FTA unlock immense potential, it is the clarity of structure and the calibre of the people involved that transform opportunity into sustained success. Working with him is more than a legal engagement; it is an experience marked by professional integrity, seamless hospitality, and strategic clarity.

For any business looking to enter or expand in the Indian market, his guidance is not just an asset; it is a necessity.

Kristin Lapajian

Attorney and Professor, Haifa, Israel

A respected Israeli legal professional, professor, and family law expert, bringing valuable international perspective, practical legal insight, and strong cross-border understanding.

Rahul constantly impresses me with his knowledge, integrity, global vision, and even his Formula 1 Racing expertise. Every conversation with him brings valuable insights and learning. I also deeply admire his generosity in creating and sharing opportunities with his entire team and the professional community.

Luz Elena Tobón

Immigration Lawyer & Partner, LCT Consulting, S.C., Mexico City, Mexico

A respected immigration law professional with strong international experience in cross-border mobility, immigration advisory, and global legal networks.

Rahul is a thoughtful and reliable professional, with a clear understanding of cross-border legal and business dynamics. My interactions with him have always reflected seriousness, practical insight, and a constructive approach to international collaboration. I am confident that his work will offer real value to businesses seeking to understand, enter and operate in India.

Marco Bertossi

Lawyer, Bertossi & Associates, Buenos Aires, Argentina

A distinguished Argentine lawyer with a practical outlook on international legal relationships and business-facing advisory.

I have had the opportunity to interact with Rahul Hingmire on matters involving business structuring and legal strategy, and I have always found his approach highly practical, commercially sound, and deeply insightful. Rahul combines strong legal expertise with a clear understanding of how businesses actually operate, making his guidance particularly valuable for companies navigating cross-border transactions and regulatory environments in India. His ability to simplify complex legal and commercial issues into actionable business decisions is truly commendable.

Dr. Mukul Shastry

Group General Counsel, Cube Highways, Noida, India

A senior legal leader known for his deep experience in infrastructure, transactions, disputes, governance, and board-level legal strategy.

Rahul Hingmire combines in-depth legal expertise in international agreements with a practical understanding of business realities. His advice is clear, commercially sound, and focused on solutions that work effectively in cross-border practice.

For companies entering the Indian market or structuring their operations in India, his perspective offers real value.

Mykola Bliashyn

Attorney, Mykola Bliashyn Law Firm, Rivne, Ukraine

A committed Ukrainian legal professional bringing resilience, practical legal insight, and strong international professional perspective.

Rahul has always stood out to me, not only as a close friend from the University of Nottingham, but also as a sharp and commercially astute mind who brings rare clarity to complex legal and business matters. In India, Restructured, he distils his deep experience as a commercial lawyer and Managing Partner at VLLP into a work that is both practical and forward-looking. The book reflects his nuanced understanding of cross-border trade dynamics and offers a structured, accessible lens for European businesses seeking to engage with the rapidly evolving Indian market. It is not just a guide to the EU–India Free Trade Agreement, but a thoughtful roadmap shaped by real-world insight, strategic thinking, and Rahul's trademark precision.

Rahul Gupta

Senior Legal Counsel, Foodics, Pune, India & Riyadh, Saudi Arabia

An experienced in-house legal counsel with strong exposure to technology, commercial contracts, and cross-border business operations across India and the Middle East.

Rahul is a great communicator, well experienced in his work and advises clients and colleagues. Great to have you as our working colleague from India.

Sim Wen Yee

Founder & Business Partner, SIM & RAHMAN, Kuala Lumpur, Malaysia

A respected Malaysian legal professional with strong expertise in succession, inheritance laws, practical advisory, and cross-border professional relationships.

India offers extraordinary opportunities, but entering such a large, dynamic, and complex market requires more than ambition. It requires a trusted advisor with deep professional resources, practical judgment, and a clear understanding of compliance realities. Rahul Hingmire is not only a good friend of mine, but also someone I regard as trustworthy, thoughtful, and highly capable.

For businesses seeking to explore India, Rahul can be a reliable partner in dealing with the jungle of legal, regulatory, and compliance challenges, allowing entrepreneurs and executives to focus their energy where it matters most: identifying and pursuing real business opportunities.

Stefan Huang

Associate Professor, National Taipei University of Business, Taipei City, Taiwan

A respected academic professional bringing strong insight into business education, global learning, and cross-border knowledge exchange.

Insightful and practical. Rahul isn't just a legal expert but also a seasoned businessman who knows what his clients will ask before they actually do and so he can anticipate and guide them through the issues without hassles.

Wayu Suthisarnsuntorn

Senior Partner, Dentons Pisut, Bangkok, Thailand

A senior Thai legal professional with strong experience in commercial advisory, cross-border matters, and international legal practice.

When our client in the education sector invested in an Indian startup, we engaged Rahul's law firm to handle the legal due diligence, documentation of the Share Subscription Agreement (SSA), and other related instruments. Rahul's team accurately identified key legal risks, stayed on schedule, and guided us at every step until closing. Their work was so impressive that I genuinely felt like hiring their lawyers myself.

Yuki Nakamura

Founder, Nakamura Law Offices, Tokyo, Japan

A respected Japanese legal professional with strong experience in business law, international advisory, and cross-border professional relationships.

Rahul is super intelligent, smart, visionary, and a great leader. His thoughts have always given me the impression of a person who can build a futuristic organisation and environment in the fields of legal, compliance, and governance, with gold standards that people will appreciate for the next 10 years and even for generations to come. I consider it my privilege to have met Rahul, who is undoubtedly one of the greatest and most distinguished minds of our country and the legal fraternity.

Zameer Nathani

Global General Counsel, DNEG, Mumbai, India

A distinguished legal leader at DNEG (the Oscar-winning global VFX, animation and production powerhouse), known for his strong experience in media, technology, AI, IP, governance, and corporate legal strategy.

Preface

The India–EU Free Trade Agreement did not arrive in calm times. It arrived in a world where European supply chains have been fractured by conflict, sanctions, energy insecurity and maritime disruption. The Red Sea crisis had already added serious pressure to the Europe–Asia shipping routes, extending transit timelines, pushing freight costs higher and forcing companies to reconsider routes that were once treated as commercially routine. More recently, renewed tension involving the United States and Iran, coupled with uncertainty around the Strait of Hormuz and the wider Gulf region, has reinforced a difficult but unavoidable lesson for European businesses: global trade is no longer protected by efficiency alone. It now depends on resilience, legal structuring, geopolitical awareness and the ability to move quickly when established corridors become exposed.

Against that background, a comprehensive trade agreement with a large, stable, democratic economy outside the primary geopolitical fault lines is not merely commercially attractive. It is strategically significant in a way that tariff schedules alone do not capture. For European boards, India is no longer only a growth market. It is increasingly a risk-balancing market, a supply-chain alternative, a manufacturing partner, a service base, a technology market and a long-term commercial platform. The FTA must therefore be read not only as a trade document, but as part of a larger boardroom response to a world where shipping lanes, sanctions, energy prices and geopolitical alliances can alter commercial assumptions almost overnight.

This book is written at a moment when that significance shifts from policy conversation into commercial obligation. For more than a decade, European boards could treat India as a horizon market –

attractive, important, but not always requiring immediate structuring decisions. That comfort has now reduced. The FTA changes the calculation. Tariff schedules are being defined, service commitments are being shaped, regulatory pathways are becoming clearer, and companies that act early will be better placed than those that wait for the market to become crowded. The question for European businesses is no longer whether to engage India seriously, but whether they are legally, commercially and operationally structured to do so effectively.

The urgency is not theoretical. When a shipping route is delayed, a sanction regime changes, a payment corridor becomes sensitive, a war-risk premium rises, or a supply chain becomes dependent on a vulnerable geography, the impact is not limited to the logistics department. It reaches pricing, contracts, working capital, customer commitments, insurance, financing, dispute risk and board accountability. In that sense, the India–EU FTA arrives at a moment when trade strategy and legal strategy have become inseparable. Businesses that treat India as a simple tariff opportunity will underuse the agreement. Businesses that treat it as a structured market-entry, supply-chain and investment opportunity will extract far greater value.

The analysis in this book is shaped by direct involvement in cross-border transactions between Europe and India – not as an observer, but as a practitioner. Structuring foreign direct investments into Indian operating entities, negotiating commercial agreements across manufacturing, technology, pharmaceuticals, and services, advising on regulatory approvals, managing disputes, and working through exits when India relationships come under pressure. Those engagements show a pattern that market analysis alone does not reveal: the businesses that succeed in India are not the most ambitious or best-capitalised. They are the most structured. The businesses that struggle have usually entered too quickly, relied on informal arrangements, underestimated state-level complexity, or treated legal compliance as an afterthought rather than a commercial instrument.

India is a large, complex, federal economy whose regulatory framework rewards seriousness and punishes informality. Its legal system is robust but not forgiving of imprecision. Companies that integrate legal thinking into commercial planning from the outset – choosing entry models for enforceability, drafting contracts for Indian courts and Indian realities, securing approvals in the correct sequence, and building compliance into operations rather than retrofitting it later – find the market far more predictable than its reputation suggests. Companies that assume the FTA alone secures their position, without aligning domestic compliance, contract discipline, tax structuring, employment obligations, data requirements, sectoral permissions and enforcement planning, tend to find themselves exposed at precisely the moment when their India operations begin to scale.

The FTA changes the policy framework. It does not change the legal work required to operate within it. Treaty benefits are not self-executing. They are realised through domestic legal systems, proper documentation, regulatory filings, contractual precision, customs compliance, rules of origin discipline, payment structuring and dispute-resolution planning. In India, that engagement requires precision from the beginning. A missed approval, vague contract, informal distributor arrangement, weak exit clause, poorly drafted arbitration provision or incomplete compliance framework can dilute the commercial advantage that the FTA was intended to create.

This book explains what that precision looks like across market entry, trade execution, compliance, contracts, sector-specific regulation, dispute resolution and exit. It is not a policy guide. It is a decision framework, written to be useful at the moment when a choice must be made – before the structure is committed, before the contract is signed, before capital is deployed, before the supply chain is shifted, before the dispute arises.

The businesses that act now, before market positions consolidate and before early-mover advantage closes, will find that the legal and commercial infrastructure built in this period compounds in value over time. The FTA does not wait. Neither does the market it opens. In a world where trade corridors can be disrupted, energy prices can move sharply, and geopolitical risk can enter the boardroom without notice, structured India entry is no longer a long-term option. It is a present commercial decision.

Who This Book is for

This book is written for European businesses and professionals who approach India as a serious, long-term strategic decision, rather than a speculative one. Its primary audience is European business leaders, board members, founders, and senior executives evaluating India entry, trade, or investment under the Free Trade Agreement (FTA). It is for those who need analysis that is legally credible, commercially grounded, and directly applicable to real decisions—not a general regulatory overview.

More specifically, this book is written for:

1. **European business leaders and boards**

   Evaluating India as a market, manufacturing base, sourcing destination, services hub, investment opportunity, or strategic partner under the FTA.

2. **Founders, promoters and senior executives**

   Considering India entry through subsidiaries, joint ventures, distribution arrangements, technology partnerships, licensing models, acquisitions, or commercial alliances.

3. **General counsel and in-house legal teams**

   Preparing for India-related contracts, regulatory approvals, dispute-resolution structures, compliance frameworks, governance risks, and enforceability issues.

4. **Chief financial officers, tax heads and compliance officers**

   Assessing tax exposure, transfer pricing, customs implications, rules of origin, payment structures, reporting duties, and financial controls linked to India operations.

5. **Company secretaries and risk managers**

   Reviewing corporate governance, board approvals, statutory filings, internal controls, compliance calendars, and India-specific operational risks.

6. **M&A advisers, private equity professionals and venture capital investors**

   Evaluating India acquisitions, minority investments, control transactions, exit structures, shareholder rights, due diligence issues, and post-closing risk.

7. **Investment bankers, family offices and fund managers**

   Looking at India as a destination for capital deployment, strategic acquisitions, distressed assets, growth investments, and sector-specific opportunities.

8. **Insolvency and restructuring professionals**

   Assessing Indian distressed assets, insolvency-driven acquisitions, resolution plans, creditor rights, turnaround opportunities, and enforcement strategy.

9. **Law firms, chambers and transaction counsel**

   Advising European clients on Indian contracts, market-entry structures, investment transactions, regulatory filings, dispute planning, and sector-specific legal issues.

10. **Cross-border consultants and trade advisers**

    Supporting businesses with India entry, foreign direct investment, customs planning, trade compliance, supply-chain restructuring, and Europe–Asia expansion strategy.

11. **Arbitration, regulatory and dispute-resolution professionals**

    Advising on contract enforceability, Indian dispute forums, arbitration clauses, interim relief, enforcement of awards, and practical dispute-prevention mechanisms.

12. **Supply-chain and strategic commercial consultants**

    Helping companies evaluate India as a sourcing, manufacturing, logistics, distribution, or regional business platform.

This book is for those who understand that India requires preparation rather than improvisation, and that the businesses that succeed there are not the most eager; they are the most structured.

Gratitude Page

Life Partner

My deepest personal gratitude goes to Mrs. Supriya Shete Hingmire, my wife, my strongest support system, and an entrepreneur in her own right. Through her work in recruitment and hiring through her business, 'Sterling Workforce Enterprises Pvt. Ltd.', and her religious experience travel venture, 'The Calling Yatra', she has shown strong people's understanding, planning ability, and execution strength. Her support has helped me think, plan, and act with greater clarity.

Parental Blessings

My deepest gratitude goes to my parents—my mother, Mrs. Hemlata Bapurao Patil, and my father, Mr. Narendra K. Hingmire—for their love, sacrifices, support, and grounding. Their values, hard work, and faith in me have given me the confidence to take risks, stay focused, and continue building this journey with humility and responsibility.

Institutional Pillars

I sincerely thank my partners, colleagues, ex-colleagues, and everyone at Vis Legis Law Practice, Advocates. I especially thank Mr. Nihaar Thackeray, Co-Founder and Co-Managing Partner at Vis Legis Law Practice, Advocates, with whom I followed the dream of starting this firm and continue to build it further. I also sincerely acknowledge Mr. Harshvardhan Deshmukh, my classmate turned Partner at the firm, whose sincerity, energy, and commitment have added meaningful strength to our professional journey; Mr. Chirag Bhavsar, Associate Partner, who is deeply committed to process, discipline, and results, and has consistently contributed to strengthening the firm's execution standards, client delivery, and matter management; and Ms. Neha Doshi, Associate Partner, who recently joined us and has taken up outreach activities and representation of our firm at global associations. I also thank our talented young attorneys—Mr. Shripad Kambli, Mr. Anand Jagmalani, and Ms. Amruta Aatre—for their commitment, sincerity, and valuable contribution to the firm's legal work, client matters, and professional growth. Their contribution, competence, and commitment have helped us handle serious legal work, cross-border transactions, litigation matters, and complex situations for domestic and international clients.

Execution Pillars

I also sincerely thank Ms. Hridika Ahire, Research Executive and Content Manager, for being a strong support system and excellent coordinator in this book journey, from planning to coordination with the publishing team. Her creative inputs, follow-ups, and commitment have added great value. I also thank Ms. Divya Jadhav, my executive assistant and constant support system, who manages countless important things with quiet efficiency. My sincere appreciation also goes to Ms. Ashwini Kasare, an excellent process coordinator, who helped expand the reach of my earlier book across Mumbai, Pune, Thane, and Navi Mumbai.

Entrepreneurial Allies

I also thank Mrs. Monica Gupta, Mr. Naren Patel, Mr. Nimit Shah, and Mr. Sudhir Mehta, for their trust, business thinking, and entrepreneurial energy, which have helped in shaping new ideas, investment discussions, and long-term opportunities. Their presence has added strength to my professional and entrepreneurial journey, especially through Earlyseed Ventures Pvt. Ltd., where they play a leading role and I remain grateful to contribute in my own small way.

Guiding Mentors

I remain deeply grateful to my networks, forums, seniors, and mentors, including Mr. Mohan Jayakar, Mr. Ameet Hariani, Mr. Dinesh Pednekar, and Mr. Kaushik Moitra, who have been my legal gurus, and Mr. Bhavook Tripathi and Mr. AgneloRajesh Athaide, who have been my business mentors. Their guidance, encouragement, wisdom, and belief in my journey have helped me at different stages of my professional growth. They have inspired me to aim higher, think bigger, and keep improving with discipline, humility, and purpose.

I also sincerely thank my Ascent Trust Group 'Anchorz' members—Mr. Abhimanyu Asija, Mr. Aleem Merchant, Mr. Kunal Doshi, Mr. Kunal Mehta, Ms. Mihika Sampat, Mr. Ritesh Mantri, Mr. Sandeep Shah, Mr. Siddharth Jain, Mr. Paresh Sangani, and Mr. Rashesh Doshi.

They have been a constant support system for professional learning and unlearning, and their regular guidance has helped me sharpen my thinking and grow with greater clarity.

A special thanks to Mr. Aleem Merchant for his valuable inputs in refining and strengthening the book title.

Global & Local Fraternity

I would like to express my sincere gratitude to my international and Indian lawyers, friends, and fellow professionals from different parts of the world and across India. I have had the privilege of interacting with you, learning from you, assisting you, and understanding the true value of professional relationships built on trust, respect, goodwill, and long-term commitment.

I also sincerely thank the networks and forums that have helped me build meaningful professional relationships and expand my learning, including the Worldwide Independent Lawyers League (WILL), World Trade Center Organisation (WTC), EU Chamber of Commerce (EUCC), Indo-Italian Chamber of Commerce and Industry (IICCI), Indo-German Chamber of Commerce (IGCC), Maharashtra Chamber of Commerce, Industry and Agriculture (MACCIA) , Bombay Chamber of Commerce and Industry (BCCI), ASCENT Foundation, and Saturday Club Global Trust (SCGT) – Elite Group, Mumbai Chapter.

Disclaimer

This book is intended to provide general information and strategic insight on the EU–India Free Trade Agreement and related legal, regulatory, and commercial considerations. It is written for educational and guidance purposes only.

Nothing in this book constitutes legal, tax, regulatory or professional advice. The content does not create a lawyer-client relationship, nor should it be relied upon as a substitute for specific advice tailored to particular facts or circumstances.

Laws, regulations, policies and enforcement practices in India and the European Union are subject to change and may vary based on sector, location and transaction structure. Readers are strongly encouraged to seek independent professional advice before making any business, legal or investment decisions.

The author and publisher disclaim all liability arising from reliance on the information contained in this book.

Contents

SECTION VIII WHAT IF THINGS GO WRONG?

SECTION IX HOW DO WE PREPARE PROPERLY?

ARE WE TRULY READY TO ENTER INDIA?

PRACTICAL TOOLS

SECTION I

WHY SHOULD WE LOOK AT INDIA?

This section sets the strategic foundation before any legal structure is considered. It explores why India has moved to the centre of EU boardroom discussions, what the India–EU FTA realistically changes, and how different European economies benefit in different ways. Rather than presenting opportunity as hype, the chapters ahead examine timing, policy intent, and market realities that shape whether India is a short-term expansion or a long-term strategic play. The most expensive mistakes in India entry do not happen during execution, they happen at this stage, when the strategic framing is set and the commitments that follow from it are made.

Chapter 1

Why is India Important for EU Businesses Right Now?

Market size, growth trajectory, geopolitical context, and why timing is a commercial decision.

The India Moment

India today is a 1.4 billion-person economy, the largest population base in the world and one of the fastest-growing major markets. Nearly 650 million people are already part of the middle or aspirational consumer class, and close to two-thirds of the population is under the age of 35. This combination of scale, consumption, and workforce depth is unmatched among large economies.

When this market is viewed together with the European Union, the picture becomes even more striking. India and the EU together connect almost 2 billion people and represent roughly one-quarter of global GDP. Even before the India–EU Free Trade Agreement, bilateral trade crossed €140-150 billion annually. With tariff elimination or phased reduction across 96-99% of traded goods, early projections suggest EU exports to India could double over the next decade.

For European businesses, this is no longer a future opportunity.

It is a present-day strategic decision.

The question European boards should now be asking is not whether India matters – that has been established. The question is whether their business has the right structure, the right contracts, and the right local understanding to convert the FTA's benefits into real commercial outcomes. Every quarter of delay is a quarter in which competitors, particularly from Asia-Pacific economies that have been active in India for longer, deepen distributor relationships, build brand recognition, and establish pricing positions that become progressively harder to displace.

The FTA has created a defined window of early-mover advantage. Companies that enter India now, with FTA-level economics, but before the Indian market positions fully consolidate, gain a compounding advantage. Those that wait for complete certainty before acting often find that the markets they intended to enter have already been claimed by more decisive competitors. In a market of India's scale and trajectory, being two to three years ahead in establishing presence, trust, and operational infrastructure represents a durable commercial advantage.

"India is no longer a future market. It is a current board-level decision."

India Has Changed Faster Than Its Reputation

For many European executives, India has always carried promise. Large numbers, strong growth and long-term potential were never in doubt. What held companies back was uncertainty—around regulation, enforcement, contracts, timelines and execution.

That hesitation is understandable.

But it is increasingly outdated.

India today does not operate like the India many EU boards remember from 10 or 15 years ago. While challenges remain, the system has become more structured, more digitised, and more predictable. Company incorporation is faster. Tax and compliance systems are largely online. Insolvency and restructuring frameworks exist where none existed earlier. Arbitration is more widely used. Contract discipline has improved.

India is no longer just an "emerging market" in how it functions. In practice, it behaves like a large, complex operating economy, similar in complexity, though different in form, to the EU itself.

For EU businesses, this shift matters. It changes how India should be evaluated: not as a distant export destination, but as a place to operate, invest and build long-term value.

> ***"India should be evaluated as an operating geography, not just an export destination."***

The Global Context Has Forced a Re-Think

The renewed interest in India is not happening in isolation. It is a response to global realities that EU companies cannot ignore.

Over the last few years, European businesses have faced:

- Trade uncertainty and tariff volatility in major markets
- Supply-chain disruptions and geopolitical risk
- Rising costs in traditional manufacturing hubs
- Pressure to diversify sourcing and production

In this environment, India offers something rare: scale with optionality. It allows companies to serve a large domestic market while also acting as a manufacturing or services base. Its internal demand provides a cushion against global slowdowns. Its policy direction has remained relatively stable compared to many peer economies.

As a result, India is increasingly seen not as a backup plan, but as a second growth engine.

What War, Sanctions and Route Disruption Have Already Changed

The conflict in Ukraine has not only disrupted European supply chains, but has forced a fundamental reassessment of where critical inputs come from and which partners can be relied upon. Sanctions regimes have made certain trade relationships legally impossible and commercially unreliable. The Red Sea crisis has added freight volatility, extended transit times by 10 to 14 days on key Europe–Asia routes, and increased landed costs across multiple supply corridors. Together, these events have done something that years of strategy consulting could not: they have made supply-chain resilience an urgent board priority rather than a long-term aspiration.

India's role in this reassessment is increasingly clear. It is not exposed to the primary geopolitical fracture lines that affect Central Asian, Middle Eastern, and Eastern European supply routes. Its democratic governance structure, rule-of-law framework, and alignment with global economic openness make it a qualitatively different risk profile compared to other large manufacturing and sourcing destinations. EU companies that had previously considered India 'too complex' are now comparing that complexity against the very real instability of their existing supply relationships. In that comparison, India's complexity appears manageable; the alternatives appear precarious.

The India–EU FTA was negotiated against this background. It is not coincidental that talks accelerated precisely when European supply-chain vulnerability became most visible. The agreement is partly a trade instrument and partly a strategic positioning document between two large democratic economies that share an interest in a rules-based international order. For EU businesses, this context is commercially significant: the FTA is supported by political will on both sides, which makes its implementation more durable and its commitments more credible than those made in purely transactional trade negotiations.

> ***"India is increasingly viewed as a second growth engine, not a contingency plan."***

What the India–EU FTA Actually Changes

The India–EU Free Trade Agreement must be understood correctly. It is not a magic solution, and it is not a shortcut. It is best described as a confidence framework.

The FTA does three important things for EU businesses.

First, it reduces cost friction. Tariff elimination or phased reduction across most goods improves price competitiveness for EU exports into India.

Second, it improves predictability. Clearer rules around trade, customs cooperation and regulatory dialogue reduce sudden surprises.

Third, it signals long-term intent. A trade agreement negotiated over many years shows that both sides want sustained economic engagement, not short-term transactions.

What the FTA does not do is remove the need for proper planning. Regulatory approvals, market-entry structuring, contract adaptation, and compliance remain critical. Businesses that assume the FTA alone guarantees success often underestimate the work required.

India is Not One Market—and That is a Strength

A common mistake EU companies make at an early stage is assuming India operates like a single, uniform market. It does not.

India is better understood as a group of markets within one country:

- Different states with different administrative cultures
- Sector-specific regulators, with varying approaches
- Regional differences in consumers, labour and execution speed

This complexity does not make India unmanageable. It makes it context-driven. Companies that recognise this early, adapt faster, and make better decisions.

India rewards businesses that invest time in understanding local realities. Those who expect uniformity often face delays and friction.

Why EU Companies Are Re-Evaluating India Now

Across Europe, different economies approach India with different motivations.

Manufacturing-heavy countries view India as a production base and supply-chain hub. Consumer-focused economies see a fast-growing premium market. Digital and services-led countries see talent, technology and scale.

"For many EU boards, India has moved from a five-year plan to a current agenda item."

Despite these differences, one question has become common across EU boardrooms:

If not now, when?

The combination of India's domestic growth and the India–EU FTA has moved India from a long-term idea to an immediate strategic discussion.

Why Past India Experiences Should Not Decide Future Strategy

Many European executives carry memories of India marked by slow processes, paperwork and uncertainty. Some of these challenges still exist, and many have changed significantly.

India today offers digital compliance systems, clearer insolvency mechanisms and a more structured regulatory environment. Enforcement still takes time, but it is more predictable than it was a decade ago.

The real risk today is not India itself.

It is entering India with old assumptions.

India Rewards Commitment, Not Experiments

India is not a market that rewards casual entry. EU companies that succeed usually commit management attention, invest early in compliance, adapt contracts properly, and build long-term relationships.

Those who struggle often rely on copied templates, weak local partners, or unrealistic timelines.

India does not promise speed.

It promises scale for those who are prepared and patient.

Why Advisers Matter More in India

India is execution-sensitive. Regulation is sector-driven. Documentation matters. Structure determines outcomes.

This is why lawyers, tax advisers and consultants play a deeper role in India than in many EU jurisdictions. A well-advised entry prevents years of corrective work later.

This book is written for businesses and their advisers because success in India is rarely accidental.

India as a Platform, Not a Project

India delivers the most value when treated as a long-term platform rather than a short-term project. EU companies that integrate India into their global strategy, rather than treating it as a side market, build resilience and scale.

"India works best when treated as a platform, not a project."

What does treating India as a platform actually mean in practice? It means entering with a legal entity that can expand, not one designed only for initial trading. It means contracting with Indian counterparties in a way that supports long-term commercial relationships, not just individual transactions. It means building a compliance infrastructure that scales with growth rather than needing to be rebuilt at every stage. It means employing or developing local expertise that accumulates institutional knowledge about the market, its customers, its regulatory patterns, and its commercial culture.

Companies that treat India as a platform make different decisions from the start. They choose subsidiary structures over distribution arrangements when the economics permit. They invest in local legal and tax advice as a strategic cost, not an overhead. They build relationships with regulators, business associations, and industry bodies rather than operating in isolation. They set realistic 5-year - to 10-year timelines for market development rather than expecting India to deliver returns in the first two years. These decisions compound.

A business that has spent five years building India as a platform will be disproportionately better positioned than one that spent five years treating it as a project.

The India–EU FTA strengthens the case for the platform approach. As tariff barriers reduce and service access expands, the business case for deeper India engagement improves materially. The FTA does not make India easy, but it makes the return on building it properly significantly better. For EU boards evaluating India, the right framing is not 'how much can we extract from this market in three years,' but rather 'what position do we need to be in when this market reaches its full potential, and what decisions do we need to take today to get there.'

India–EU Opportunity at a Glance

1. India population: about ~1.47 billion (2026)
2. EU population: about ~449 million (2026)
3. Combined market size: about ~1.9 billion people
4. India population under 35: about 65%
5. EU–India trade in goods: €120 billion (2024)
6. EU–India trade in services: €59.7 billion (2023)
7. FTA coverage: tariff elimination or reduction covering 96.6% of EU goods exports to India by value
8. Export potential: EU goods exports to India are expected to double by 2032
9. Combined GDP: about 21% of global GDP on a nominal/current US$ basis, using 2024 World Bank data
10. India services sector: about 55% of India's GVA / economy
11. India FDI point: better stated as India remains a major global FDI destination, with about $27.6 billion in FDI inflows in 2024, rather than using a vague "top global destination" line

12. Middle / aspirational consumers: keep this only as an estimate, not a hard fact, unless you want to cite a specific market-study source; ~650 million is usable as a directional business estimate, but I would not present it as an official statistic.

Five EU Countries With Natural Advantage in India

The India–EU FTA does not create relationships from scratch. It strengthens existing ones. Several EU countries already have deep, historical trade and industrial links with India, which the FTA now makes more efficient.

1. **Germany** has been a long-standing partner in engineering, machinery, automotive components, chemicals, and medical devices. These sectors align directly with India's manufacturing and infrastructure priorities.
2. **France** combines strong government-to-government engagement with private-sector presence in aerospace, energy, luxury goods, cosmetics, and pharmaceuticals. The FTA supports scaling in high-value goods and services.
3. **Italy's** relationship with India is driven largely by SMEs. Italian machinery, textiles, fashion, and food products already have recognition in India. Tariff reductions directly benefit these categories.
4. **The Netherlands** has long acted as a trade and investment gateway. Its strengths in logistics, chemicals, electronics, and holding structures align well with India's supply-chain ambitions.
5. **Belgium**, often understated, has deep ties through diamonds, pharmaceuticals, chemicals, and life sciences. Regulatory cooperation under the FTA strengthens this niche trade.

> ***"The FTA does not create winners, it accelerates those already positioned to win."***

India is no longer a future option. It is a present strategic decision. The India–EU FTA lowers friction, but success still depends on structure, contracts, compliance, and long-term thinking.

EU businesses that prepare well will find scale.

Those that enter casually will find friction.

Chapter 2

What Does India–EU FTA Actually Change for Us?

What the FTA delivers, where its limits are, and how boards should interpret it.

Clearing the Biggest Misunderstanding

The India–EU Free Trade Agreement has created strong momentum across European boardrooms. Headlines speak of tariff elimination, market access, and a new phase of commercial cooperation. For many businesses, that creates a simple assumption: the FTA makes India easier.

That assumption is partly correct and partly dangerous.

The FTA changes the commercial framework between India and the European Union in important ways. At the same time, it does not remove many of the legal, regulatory and operational realities that determine whether an Indian entry succeeds or fails. This chapter explains what the FTA changes, what it does not change, and how EU businesses should read it before making decisions.

> ***"The FTA reduces friction, but it does not remove responsibility."***

1. What the FTA Changes

1. Tariff Reduction Becomes the New Baseline

The most visible change under the India–EU FTA is tariff reduction. Across most covered goods, duties are either reduced or eliminated over a phased period.

"Lower tariffs improve competitiveness, not profitability by default."

For EU exporters, that means:

- better price competitiveness in India
- stronger margin flexibility
- greater long-term pricing predictability

But lower tariffs do not mean lower total cost by default. Logistics, certification, customs compliance, local taxes, and contractual design still matter.+

2. Tariff Reductions Must Flow Into Contracts

One of the most underestimated FTA issues is the link between tariff changes and contract drafting. When tariffs reduce, pricing clauses in distribution, supply, and purchase contracts are directly affected, but only if those contracts are built to absorb the change.

A fixed-price distribution agreement may stop the exporter from using tariff savings to gain market share. On the other hand, passing through all tariff savings immediately may leave no protection if origin benefits are later denied. Tariff changes, therefore, need to be reflected in:

- pricing review mechanisms
- landed-cost calculations
- origin-risk allocation
- import cost clauses
- change-in-law provisions

These are not drafting refinements. They affect whether the FTA improves profitability or creates later disputes.

3. Trade Becomes More Predictable, Not Simpler

The FTA improves predictability by strengthening customs cooperation, institutional dialogue, and trade treatment visibility. That matters because predictability supports:

- longer planning horizons

- stronger supply-chain decisions
- more reliable commercial contracts

But predictability does not mean uniform application. Indian customs and regulators will still expect complete documentation and defensible compliance.

2. Rules of Origin: The Gatekeeper of FTA Benefits

FTA benefits apply only if goods qualify as originating under the agreement. That is not automatic.

For EU businesses, origin compliance means:

- origin thresholds must actually be met
- value-addition calculations must be correct
- supplier documentation must be current
- manufacturing steps must be traceable
- certificates must match the shipment properly

In complex EU supply chains, this becomes a serious commercial issue. A product may genuinely qualify in substance and still lose FTA benefit if the documentation cannot prove it.

Why Documentation Discipline Matters

FTA benefit is not delivered by treaty text alone. It is delivered by records that can survive customs scrutiny. Indian customs authorities can question origin retrospectively through post-clearance audit. A business that cannot produce coherent origin files, supplier declarations, and calculation support may face:

- full duty reassessment
- interest exposure
- penalty risk
- disruption across prior shipments

This is why origin compliance must be built before the first shipment, not after the first audit notice.

3. What the FTA Does Not Change

1. The FTA Does Not Override Indian Domestic Law

A free trade agreement does not replace Indian law. It operates above the trade relationship, not instead of domestic regulation.

Indian rules on:

- company formation
- tax
- labour and employment
- environment
- licensing
- sector regulation

continue to apply fully.

> ***"An FTA does not replace domestic law, it sits above it."***

2. Market Entry Still Requires Structure and Approval

The FTA does not give EU companies an automatic right to operate in India. Depending on sector and business model, entry may still require:

- FDI approvals
- sectoral licences
- regulatory registrations
- local entity formation

The agreement improves the environment for trade and investment. It does not remove regulatory gates.

3. Services Access Remains Regulated

The FTA may improve the framework for services trade, but local licensing, data rules, tax exposure, and sector regulation continue to apply. Permanent establishment risk does not disappear. Data localisation issues do not disappear. Regulatory oversight does not disappear.

4. Enforcement Reality Remains the Same

The FTA does not change how Indian courts or arbitral tribunals function. Enforcement timelines, procedural discipline and forum strategy still matter.

That means:

- arbitration planning still matters
- governing law still matters
- seat selection still matters
- interim relief strategy still matters

"The FTA does not change enforcement reality, planning does."

4. Why the FTA Still Matters

If the FTA does not remove regulation, compliance, or enforcement complexity, why does it matter so much?

Because it changes the baseline.

Before the FTA:

- tariffs created uncertainty
- policy direction was less settled
- long-term India planning carried more friction

After the FTA:

- cost structures are clearer
- commercial engagement is more credible
- long-term planning is easier to justify

The FTA does not eliminate work; it makes the work more worthwhile.

5. How the FTA Should Change Decision-Making

The FTA should change commercial thinking in four practical ways.

- **Pricing Must Be Re-Modelled**

  Products that were previously uncompetitive in India may now need fresh pricing analysis based on reduced tariffs, origin cost, freight pressure, and distributor economics.

- **Timing Must Be Reconsidered**

  Some businesses delayed India entry because the commercial numbers did not work. In a post-FTA environment, those same numbers may now justify entry.

- **Structure Must Be Re-Evaluated**

  Reduced import costs may support a more direct commercial presence in India. Distributor, subsidiary, joint venture or hybrid models should all be tested again under post-FTA economics.

- **Planning Horizons Must Expand**

  The FTA moves India from a speculative market to a strategic one. It deserves corresponding board attention, capital allocation, and management seriousness.

6. What Has Already Changed Before Full FTA Operation

Even before the FTA fully operates, the global trade environment has already changed. The Ukraine conflict, sanctions exposure, and Red Sea shipping disruption have materially affected EU–India trade economics.

For EU businesses, this means:

- freight costs remain volatile
- delivery timelines are less stable

- sanctions screening is essential
- landed-cost modelling must go beyond tariff assumptions

The practical lesson is clear: India's strategy must be built on both **FTA benefits** and **real-world disruption risks**. The FTA improves the framework, but logistics, compliance, and sanctions still shape the final commercial result.

Common Mistakes EU Businesses Make at This Stage

- assuming tariff cuts equal ease of entry
- ignoring Rules of Origin
- using unmodified EU contracts
- underestimating compliance planning

These mistakes are avoidable.

What This Chapter Means for EU Businesses

The India–EU FTA:

- reduces tariff friction
- improves predictability
- signals long-term commercial intent

But it does not:

- remove domestic regulation
- replace contract discipline
- guarantee enforcement outcomes

The FTA is a tool, not a shortcut. Its value depends on how well businesses structure, document, and execute around it.

"The FTA gives direction. Execution still determines results."

Chapter Takeaway

Most post-FTA problems do not arise from the agreement itself. They arise from misreading what the agreement actually does. Businesses that treat the FTA as a framework for disciplined India entry usually improve outcomes. Businesses that treat it as a substitute for legal and commercial preparation usually create avoidable problems.

Chapter 3

Which EU Countries and Industries Benefit the Most

How Germany, France, Italy, the Netherlands, the Nordics, CEE and other economies gain differently.

One Agreement. Very Different Outcomes.

The India–EU Free Trade Agreement applies uniformly to all EU member states. Yet, investment outcomes will not be uniform. History, sector alignment and capital behaviour matter far more than treaty text.

Before the FTA, EU investment into India was already meaningful. In 2013, EU equity FDI into India stood at approximately USD 5.0 billion annually. By 2024, this figure had more than doubled to USD 11.7 billion per year. This growth occurred without the FTA in force.

The FTA does not create this trajectory.

It accelerates it.

Germany: Manufacturing Depth Meets FTA Cost Efficiency

Germany has been one of India's most consistent industrial partners for decades. Even before 2014, German capital was deeply embedded in Indian automotive manufacturing, machinery, chemicals, electrical equipment and industrial engineering.

This historical presence matters.

EU cumulative FDI data shows that automobiles (~USD 9.3 bn), chemicals (~USD 6.2 bn), and services (~USD 18.2 bn) are among the top recipient sectors of EU investment into India. These are precisely the sectors where German companies dominate.

By 2024-25, Germany continues to be a core industrial investor, benefiting from:

- Reduced tariffs on machinery and components
- Greater predictability for long-cycle manufacturing projects
- Localisation incentives aligned with Make in India policies

Looking ahead to 2034-35, German FDI into India is expected to grow 2–3× from current levels, driven by:

- EV and auto-component localisation
- Energy transition equipment
- Industrial automation and advanced manufacturing

Integrated Insight:

Germany does not benefit because the FTA exists. Germany benefits because it was already aligned with India's industrial future.

France: Capital-Intensive Sectors With Strategic Backing

French investment into India has historically been concentrated in aerospace, energy, defence-linked manufacturing, pharmaceuticals and premium consumer brands.

Before 2014, French FDI was smaller in volume than Germany's, but higher in strategic depth – often supported by long-term government-to-government engagement.

By 2024-25, EU sector data shows strong cumulative inflows into:

- Services (~USD 18.2 bn)
- Pharma-linked chemicals (~USD 6.2 bn)
- High-value manufacturing

French companies benefit disproportionately because:

- Their sectors are less price-sensitive and more trust-driven
- Tariff reduction improves margins rather than market access alone
- India's demand for aerospace, energy, and healthcare is structural

By 2034–35, French FDI is expected to expand steadily through:

- Civil aviation supply chains
- Renewable and nuclear energy projects
- Healthcare and pharma manufacturing

Integrated Insight:

France benefits because the FTA rewards capital patience, not volume aggression.

Italy: SMEs, Specialisation, and Immediate Tariff Impact

Italy's engagement with India has never been dominated by large conglomerates. It has always been SME-led, focusing on:

- Textile machinery
- Fashion and lifestyle products
- Light engineering
- Food and beverage

Before 2014, Italian FDI volumes were modest, but trade engagement was strong. Tariffs were a major friction point.

By 2024-25, EU FDI into trading (~USD 7.2 bn) and manufacturing-linked services shows where Italian firms operate most comfortably - distribution, sourcing, and niche manufacturing.

The FTA directly reduces tariffs in the exact categories where Italian SMEs compete.

By 2034-35, Italian FDI is expected to grow in a distributed pattern:

- Smaller ticket sizes
- Higher deal count
- Strong reliance on distributors, JVs, and licensing

Integrated Insight:

Italy benefits not through scale, but through precision – the FTA removes price friction from SME trade.

Netherlands: The Hidden Multiplier

The Netherlands has long been one of the largest EU sources of FDI into India, often acting as a gateway economy rather than a pure exporter.

Even before 2014, Dutch FDI flowed into India via:

- Holding structures
- Logistics and ports
- Chemicals and electronics
- Trade facilitation platforms

By 2024-25, the Netherlands continues to rank among the top investing countries, benefiting heavily from EU-wide trade expansion.

As India–EU trade volumes grow, the Netherlands gains:

- Structuring mandates
- Logistics volume
- Investment routing and consolidation

By 2034–35, Dutch-linked India investment is expected to expand significantly, even if the underlying capital originates elsewhere.

Integrated Insight:

The Netherlands wins when everyone else trades more.

Nordic Countries: Technology-First, Not Tariff-First

Nordic (Denmark, Finland, Iceland, Norway, Sweden) investment into India has historically been lower in volume but higher in strategic value. Before 2014, Nordic FDI focused on:

- Telecom and digital infrastructure
- Clean energy
- Industrial software
- Maritime and logistics services

EU cumulative FDI data shows strong inflows into:

- IT and software (~USD 12.8 bn)
- Services (~USD 18.2 bn)

These sectors align closely with Nordic strengths.

Because tariffs matter less for services and digital sectors, the FTA benefits Nordic firms mainly through:

- Regulatory dialogue
- Market confidence
- Long-term policy signalling

By 2034-35, Nordic FDI is expected to outperform in:

- Green energy
- Smart manufacturing
- Digital public infrastructure

Integrated Insight:

Nordics benefit because India's future demand is capability-driven, not price-driven.

Central and Eastern Europe (CEE): Indirect but Structural Gains

CEE countries such as **Austria**, **Poland**, **the Czech Republic**, **Slovakia**, and **Hungary** rarely appear in headline India FDI data. Yet their role is critical.

Before 2014, CEE engagement was mostly indirect—through German and French supply chains.

By 2024-25, as EU FDI into automotive and industrial manufacturing expanded, CEE manufacturers benefited as component suppliers.

By 2034-35, CEE economies are expected to gain through:

- Deeper integration into India-focused EU supply chains
- Indirect export growth
- Manufacturing spillover

Integrated Insight:

CEE benefits through integration, not visibility.

FDI Trajectory Summary

- 2013 (Pre-FTA): ~USD 5.0 bn EU FDI annually
- 2024 (Pre-Implementation): ~USD 11.7 bn annually
- 2034–35 (Base Case): ~USD 27–30 bn annually
- 2034–35 (Upside Case): ~USD 35–40 bn annually

The FTA acts as a multiplier, not a trigger.

What This Chapter Ultimately Shows

The India–EU FTA does not produce equal winners. It rewards alignment, history and preparedness. Countries that were already invested in will scale faster. Countries entering for the first time will need patience.

SECTION II

HOW DO WE ENTER INDIA?

Once interest turns into intent, structuring becomes the work. This is the moment when legal and commercial advisory engagement earns its highest value, not by confirming that India is attractive, but by designing the legal architecture that makes the attraction commercially durable. The chapters in this section address the decisions that determine whether an India entry survives first contact with regulatory reality: which entity to use, which approvals to obtain, and how to structure the investment so that control, tax exposure, and exit options remain manageable over time.

Chapter 4

What is the Best Way for an EU Company to Enter India?

Subsidiary, Joint Venture, Distributor, Franchise: what survives real operating pressure.

The entry structure decision is not a procedural step. It is the first substantive legal choice a European business makes about India, and it determines the operating conditions, compliance obligations, control dynamics, and exit options for everything that follows. Many EU companies lose years in India recovering from the wrong entry decision, one made for administrative convenience rather than commercial durability, or one that reflected the India of five years ago rather than the India that the FTA now makes accessible.

India gives EU businesses four common entry routes. None is "best" in isolation. The right structure depends on what is being sold, how regulated the sector is, how much control is needed, and how much execution capacity exists locally. But the structure also depends on something that is often underweighted: what happens when things do not go as planned. The entry model that looks cleanest on paper is frequently the one that creates the most friction in practice, because it was chosen for initial ease, not for durability under real operating pressure around pricing, compliance, distribution, service levels, people, and dispute handling.

> ***"The entry structure you choose in year one shapes the legal position you defend in year five. Choose for durability, not convenience."***

This chapter addresses that decision as a practitioner would: by examining what each structure actually delivers under real conditions, not on paper. It draws on real European entry experiences—both the ones that held together and the ones that required expensive correction—to make the analysis directly applicable to the structuring decisions that European boards and their advisers face now.

The Four Entry Models

1) Wholly Owned Subsidiary (WOS)

A local Indian company, fully owned by the EU parent (subject to sector rules). You run it, you fund it, you control it.

Best for: regulated sectors, premium brands, IP-heavy products, long-term manufacturing, services with client risk, and where quality control matters.

The hidden truth: a subsidiary reduces partner risk, but increases execution responsibility.

2) Joint Venture (JV)

You partner with an Indian company; ownership and control are shared via shareholding and shareholder agreement.

Best for: sectors needing local relationships, licensing, land, government interface, or rapid scale, where the partner truly adds value.

The hidden truth: most JV failures are not "market failures"; they are governance failures.

3) Distributor / Agent Model

You sell through an Indian distributor who imports, stocks, sells and sometimes services.

Best for: early-stage market testing, limited SKUs, standard products, and when you want speed without heavy fixed costs.

The hidden truth: distributors can scale you fast—or quietly damage your brand if contracts and controls are weak.

4) Franchise / Licence Model

You allow an Indian partner to operate under your brand, SOPs and commercial rules. Common in retail, food, education, services and consumer brands.

Best for: brands with repeatable operating models and strong training systems.

The hidden truth: Franchise success in India depends more on partner selection and audit discipline than on the brand name.

Two-Minute Decision Rule

If you want a fast first filter, use this.

- If quality, IP, safety, liability, or compliance is high → **Subsidiary**
- If local access is critical, and the partner brings real leverage → **JV**
- If you want speed with limited risk, and you can control via contract →**Distributor**
- If your business is a replicable operating format and brand is the asset →**Franchise**

"If you cannot protect your product quality and customer experience, India will punish the brand, not the partner."

Entry Model Comparison

Entry model	Control	Speed to market	Capital needed	Compliance burden	Partner risk	Best suited for
Wholly owned subsidiary	High	Medium	High	High	Low	Manufacturing, regulated sectors, premium brands, services
Joint venture	Medium	Medium	Medium	Medium–High	High	Regulated access, land-heavy projects, deep local relationships
Distributor/ Agent	Low–Medium	High	Low	Medium	Medium–High	Standard goods, early expansion, testing India
Franchise/ Licence	Medium	High	Low – Medium	Medium	High	Retail formats, lifestyle, education, food and beverage

What Works in India (And Why)

Subsidiary works when

A subsidiary is best when the business needs tight control over:

- product quality and certification
- data handling and privacy risk
- IP and know-how
- customer safety and liability
- brand reputation and premium positioning

In India, operational variance is common. A wholly owned structure lets you enforce standards. Many EU companies that sell high-value industrial goods or sensitive consumer products eventually move to a subsidiary, even if they start with a distributor.

Risk to manage: higher fixed cost, slower initial scale.

JV works when...

A JV works when the Indian partner provides a real, measurable advantage, such as:

- government interface / local permits
- land / distribution infrastructure
- installed client base
- manufacturing capability
- sector credibility

A JV fails when the partner brings only “relationships” without execution capability, or when the governance terms are vague.

Risk to manage: deadlocks, brand dilution and “step-motherly treatment” of your products inside joint sales channels (a common India JV pain point).

Distributor works when...

Distributor entry works if:

- product is standardised
- regulatory approvals are manageable
- service and spare parts are planned
- pricing discipline is enforceable by contract
- you have clear audit rights and market visibility

Distributor entry fails when:

- distributor pushes only high-margin SKUs
- service quality is poor

- distributor becomes the face of the brand and damages it
- you cannot verify import compliance and end-user practices

Franchise works when...

A franchise succeeds when:

- operating model is repeatable
- brand standards are enforceable
- training systems exist
- audits are frequent
- unit economics work for the franchisee

Franchise fails in India when franchisees treat the brand as a signboard and ignore SOPs, while the franchisor avoids conflict to keep unit count high.

Which Model Fits Which EU Industry

Industry / Sector	Model that usually wins	Why
Industrial machinery, auto components, B2B engineering	Subsidiary or strong distributor → then subsidiary	Quality + service + liability need control
Pharma, medical devices, regulated healthcare	Subsidiary (often unavoidable)	Compliance, approvals, liability, audits
Luxury / premium consumer brands	Subsidiary or franchise with tight audits	Brand control + consistency
Retail (multi-city)	Franchise or subsidiary (policy dependent)	Need scale + SOP control
Software / tech services	Subsidiary (sometimes contractor first)	Data, contracts, client risk, people
Food and beverage (consumer)	Franchise + strict compliance	Replicable format, local ops

What Usually Fails in India: Hard Truths

Common reasons entry models fail

- Wrong partner selection (values mismatch, capability mismatch)
- Weak contracts (no audit rights, weak termination, weak brand control)
- Underestimating service + spare parts + after-sales obligations
- Overestimating "distribution reach" without proof

> ***"A joint venture is not a shortcut. It is a long-term marriage with a detailed prenuptial."***

- No India decision-maker (India needs local leadership, not remote control)
- Compliance treated as paperwork instead of risk management

A key pattern is this: EU companies often choose "low control" models to reduce risk, but in India, low control can create bigger risk because the brand is still blamed.

Case Studies From Big Four Companies From EU Countries

Bosch – Start with local partnership, then deepen control

Bosch's India story is a classic example of entering a restrictive market by using the right model at the right time.

Bosch's early breakthrough in India came through a partnership and licensing approach with Motor Industries Co. Ltd. (MICO) in the early 1950s, which helped Bosch enter India during a period of restrictive foreign company policies.

Over time, Bosch expanded manufacturing and local capability. Today, it operates a deep manufacturing and engineering presence in India, which is consistent with a long-term "build in India" approach.

Why this is a success story

- Bosch did not insist on full control on day one
- It used a partnership model to enter, then steadily increased localisation and operational depth
- It aligned with India's industrial and manufacturing agenda early

Lesson for EU companies: Start with what the market allows (partnership/distribution), but plan your roadmap toward control and localisation if the sector demands it.

Philips – Long-term local presence and structured evolution

Philips began operations in India in 1930, with the establishment of Philips Electrical Co. (India) in Kolkata as a sales outlet, later building a manufacturing presence.

Philips India's longevity illustrates a core India truth: long-term winners keep adjusting structure, product strategy, and compliance posture as India changes.

Why this is a success story

- Early entry and patient scaling
- Ability to operate through regulatory changes and market shifts
- A long-term India operating mindset rather than "export-only thinking"

Lesson for EU companies: India rewards companies that treat it as a platform, not a short-term sales project.

Carrefour – Policy reality defeated the entry thesis

Carrefour entered India in 2010 and later announced it would shut its five cash-and-carry stores by the end of September 2014.

Carrefour's India model was wholesale (cash-and-carry), but the broader retail policy environment and strategic priorities did not support scale the way Carrefour needed.

Why this is a failure story:

- The business needed scale to justify the model
- India's retail policy environment and political risk remained high at that time
- The model did not reach the scale necessary to win

Lesson for EU companies: In sectors where policy is politically sensitive, you must design the entry model with policy risk, state-level variation in mind and have a clear exit plan.

Fiat – JV distribution model broke trust and performance

Fiat and Tata had a sales and distribution arrangement that was brought under a joint venture structure, including manufacturing at Ranjangaon, near Pune.

By 2012, the distribution alliance ended, and management control of Fiat's commercial and distribution activities was to be handed over to a Fiat group-owned company.

Public reporting and case documentation also noted that the joint distribution and dealership experience created issues for Fiat buyers and failed to meet expectations.

Why this is a failure story:

- JV distribution created weak brand control
- Misaligned incentives in shared showrooms hurt customer experience
- Governance and execution did not support the Fiat brand

Lesson for EU companies: If your brand depends on customer experience, a shared distribution JV can destroy trust if your product is not treated as the priority.

"In India, the wrong partner is more expensive than the wrong product."

What They Chose vs What They Learned

Company (Country)	Entry route	Outcome	What worked / failed	Lesson
Bosch (Germany)	Partnership/ licensing → deeper local build	Success	Phased entry + localisation	Enter smart, then build control
Philips (Netherlands)	Early incorporation + long-term local presence	Success	Patience + adaptation	India rewards long-term operators
Carrefour (France)	Wholesale retail presence	Exit (2014)	Policy + scale mismatch	Treat policy risk as core risk
Fiat (Italy)	JV distribution/ manufacturing with Tata	JV ended (2012)	Brand control + incentives failed	Customer experience must stay under your control

The "Model Upgrade" Strategy

Many EU companies do best with a staged plan:

Stage 1: Distributor / limited presence → learn the market

Stage 2: Subsidiary for control + key accounts

Stage 3: Local manufacturing / JV for scale where required

Stage 4: Franchise expansion (for consumer formats)

This is not indecision. This is how risk is managed in a high-potential market.

What This Chapter Means for EU Businesses

If you want to win in India, don't start with "what is easiest." Start with:

- What level of control do we need?
- What is compliance and liability exposure?
- What is the real value of a local partner?
- Can we audit and enforce standards?
- What is our exit plan if assumptions fail?

India is not a place where the entry model is a formality. It shapes everything – cost, speed, disputes, brand perception, and long-term viability.

Chapter 5

Do We Need Government Approvals or Licences in India?

FDI limits, automatic vs approval routes, sector regulators, and timeline realities.

For many EU companies, the single biggest anxiety before entering India is this:

"How many approvals will we need, and how long will they take?"

The fear is understandable. India's regulatory reputation is often described as complex, layered, and slow. The reality today is more nuanced. India does require approvals in certain sectors, but most foreign investment now comes through the automatic route, without prior government permission.

The real challenge is not the number of approvals.

It is knowing which approvals matter, when they are triggered, and who controls them.

This chapter breaks that down clearly.

The Big Picture: India's FDI Framework Today

India allows foreign direct investment (FDI) under two broad routes:

1. **Automatic Route** – no prior government approval required
2. **Government (Approval) Route** – prior approval required before investment

Over the last decade, India has steadily expanded the automatic route. Today, the majority of sectors relevant to EU businesses fall under the automatic route, either fully or up to a specified percentage.

This means:

- You do not need to negotiate with ministries for every investment
- You can incorporate and invest faster than before
- Compliance happens after investment, not before

However, this does not mean "no regulation."

It means regulation shifts from entry to operation.

Automatic Route vs Government Route

Automatic Route – What It Really Means

If your sector is under the automatic route:

- You do not need prior approval from the Indian government
- You can invest up to the permitted FDI cap
- You must comply with reporting and sectoral conditions

Most EU manufacturing, services, IT, trading, and B2B businesses fall here.

Government Route – What Triggers It

Government approval is required when:

- The sector is sensitive or strategic
- The FDI cap is limited
- There are national interest or security considerations

Approval is sought through the single-window online system, not physical files.

FDI Caps: The Second Layer of Reality

Even under the automatic route, FDI caps matter.

A sector may allow:

- 100% foreign investment
- 74% foreign investment
- 49% foreign investment

Crossing the permitted cap automatically pushes you into the approval route, even if the sector is otherwise liberalised.

This is where many EU companies make planning errors.

Key FDI Caps Relevant to EU Businesses

Sector	FDI Cap	Route
Manufacturing	100%	Automatic
IT / Software / SaaS	100%	Automatic
Wholesale trading (B2B)	100%	Automatic
Single-brand retail	100%	Automatic (conditions apply)
Multi-brand retail	Restricted	Government route
Insurance	74%	Automatic
Banking (private)	74%	Automatic
Defence manufacturing	Up to 74%	Automatic (beyond → approval)
Telecom	100%	Automatic
Pharmaceuticals (greenfield)	100%	Automatic
Pharmaceuticals (brownfield)	Up to 74%	Automatic

Note: Caps are subject to conditions and periodic updates; professional advice is essential.

Sector Regulators: The Real Gatekeepers

Many EU companies focus too much on "FDI approval" and too little on sector regulators. In practice, sector regulators often matter more than FDI policy.

Examples:

- Manufacturing may not need FDI approval, but may need environmental and factory licences
- Pharma may be automatic for FDI, but still requires drug approvals
- Fintech may allow 100% FDI, but faces regulatory scrutiny from financial regulators

FDI permission gets you into the country.

Sector regulators decide whether you can operate smoothly.

- **Common Sector Regulators EU Companies Encounter:** EU companies entering India often expect a single approval pathway. In practice, regulation is sector-driven, and multiple authorities may operate simultaneously at central and state levels. Understanding which regulator influences your sector helps avoid delays and unrealistic timelines.
- **Manufacturing and Industrial:** EU manufacturers typically engage with **state industrial development authorities**, **pollution control boards** and **factory inspectorates**. These bodies review land use, environmental permissions, safety compliance and operational readiness. Approvals may vary significantly from one state to another, making early local planning essential.
- **Pharma and Healthcare:** Healthcare businesses interact with **drug regulatory authorities**, pricing regulators, and product quality oversight bodies. Approval pathways can involve clinical data, import permissions, and ongoing compliance monitoring. Regulatory scrutiny is higher where patient safety and pricing transparency are involved.
- **Food, Beverage and Cosmetics:** Companies in consumer health and lifestyle sectors deal with **food safety regulators**, labelling authorities and import certification bodies. Packaging

disclosures, ingredient approvals and product classification often influence market-entry timelines more than tariffs.

- **Telecom, IT and Digital:** Technology companies encounter the **telecom regulator**, data governance authorities, and cybersecurity compliance frameworks. Issues around data storage, cross-border transfers, and service licensing require careful planning before contracts are signed or services are launched.
- **Financial Services and Fintech:** Banks, fintech firms, and payment platforms must work closely with **banking regulators**, securities authorities, and payment system overseers. Licensing expectations, data handling obligations, and audit culture are more structured compared to many EU jurisdictions.

Practical Reality

Each regulator operates with its own timelines, documentation standards and administrative approach. Successful EU entrants treat regulatory engagement as an ongoing process rather than a one-time approval exercise, aligning legal strategy with operational execution from the beginning.

When Approvals Are Actually Needed: Practical Triggers

EU companies usually need government approval if:

- They exceed sectoral FDI caps
- They enter restricted retail formats
- They invest in sensitive infrastructure
- They acquire existing regulated businesses
- They restructure ownership post-entry

"Most approval problems arise during expansion, not entry."

In many cases, the approval requirement is triggered later, not at entry—during expansion, acquisition, or restructuring.

What Usually Delays Approvals

Delays rarely happen because of policy. They happen because of:

- Poor documentation
- Incorrect sector classification
- Incomplete business descriptions
- Mismatch between structure and activity
- Ignoring state-level approvals

Approvals move faster when filings are precise, conservative, and well-explained.

Strategic Planning: How Smart EU Companies Reduce Approval Risk

Successful EU entrants do three things early:

1. Map FDI caps + sector rules together
2. Design entry structure within automatic limits
3. Plan future expansion without breaching caps accidentally

Many approval issues can be avoided simply by choosing the right ownership and activity mix at entry.

Entry Planning vs Approval Risk

Planning choice	Approval risk
Conservative ownership at entry	Low
Over-ambitious ownership	High
Clear activity description	Low
Vague “future business” scope	High
State-wise licence mapping	Low
Ignoring state approvals	High

Common Mistakes EU Businesses Make

- Assuming automatic route means "no rules"
- Ignoring sector regulators
- Exceeding FDI caps unintentionally
- Structuring first and asking later
- Leaving compliance to distributors

Chapter Takeaway

In India, approvals are predictable if you respect the framework. Problems arise when businesses treat India like a copy-paste jurisdiction.

Most approval issues are structural, mistakes, not policy hostility.

Chapter 6

How Should We Structure Our Investment in India?

Equity, debt, hybrids, control rights, tax exposure and exit planning from day one.

Most EU companies entering India spend significant time on whether they can invest – FDI caps, sector limits, approval routes, and regulatory permissions. Far fewer spend enough time on how they should invest.

That is a mistake.

The investment structure decision is where legal and commercial thinking must work together from the outset. Structure determines control, control determines what can be built, and what can be built determines whether the India investment actually delivers what the board approved it to deliver.

> ***"In India, structure decides outcomes long before any dispute starts."***

The Key Questions That Should Decide Your Structure

Before picking Equity, Debt, or a Hybrid, answer these key questions:

1. What is your real objective in India?
2. Market access, manufacturing base, acquisition, services delivery, or long-term platform?
3. How much control do you need?

4. Full control, shared control, or only protective rights?
5. How much capital risk can you accept?
6. Will you fund growth patiently or prefer protected returns?
7. Will you exit, or will you operate long-term?
8. Your exit horizon changes everything.
9. What is your regulatory comfort level?
10. Sector rules, pricing controls, licensing, and compliance intensity.

If these are unclear, no "best structure" exists. You will only create avoidable risk.

The Core Structures EU Companies Use

There are four common investment structures for EU companies entering India:

1. **Wholly Owned Subsidiary** (WOS) – Equity
2. **Joint Venture** – Equity with governance controls
3. **Minority Investment**, – Equity + protective rights
4. **Debt or Hybrid** – Instruments that behave like debt but sit within company law

Most Indian success stories involve a mix, rather than a single instrument.

1) Wholly Owned Subsidiary (Equity): Control-First Model

What it is

You set up an Indian company and own it fully (or up to the permitted FDI cap). The company is your operating arm in India.

When it works best

- You need strong IP and brand control
- You have regulated products or liability risk

- You need consistent service levels and audit discipline
- You are investing for five to 10 years or more

What EU companies underestimate

A wholly owned subsidiary gives control, but it also makes you responsible for:

- Compliance and Reporting
- Hiring and Labour exposure
- Tax and Permanent establishment management
- Vendor discipline and contract enforcement

"A subsidiary reduces partner risk, but it increases execution responsibility."

The benefit: you control outcomes. The cost: you must manage execution.

2) Joint Venture (Equity): Access-First Model

What it is

You invest with an Indian partner; ownership and governance are shared.

When it works best

- You need land, licences, or local access
- You need a partner's distribution channel
- You need credibility in a regulated ecosystem
- You want faster scaling without building everything from scratch

Where JV structures fail

JV failure in India is usually due to:

- vague reserved matters
- unclear decision rights
- deadlocks with no exit pathway
- incentives mismatch (partner prioritises its other businesses)

Rule: If you can't define control clearly, don't form a JV.

3) Minority Investment: Protection-First Model

What it is

You buy a minority stake (for example, 10%–49%) in an Indian company. You do not control operations, but you protect your position through shareholder rights.

When it works best

- You want exposure to India without running operations
- You are investing in a local champion
- You want a strategic partnership without full responsibility
- You plan an exit in three to seven years

Critical point

Minority investment is safe only if you negotiate:

- reserved matters
- information rights
- anti-dilution / pre-emptive rights
- exit rights (put/call, drag/tag, IPO strategy)

Without these, minority investments become "hope-based."

4) Debt and Hybrid Instruments: Return-First Model

What they are

These are instruments that provide:

- downside protection
- structured returns
- priority repayment rights

Common approaches include:

- shareholder loans (subject to rules)
- compulsorily convertible instruments (used frequently)
- optionally convertible structures (must be carefully designed)

When they work best

- You want predictable returns while retaining upside
- You want capital protection in early Indian entry
- You are funding a JV or expansion and want structured repayment

What to watch

Hybrid structures can trigger:

- regulatory classification issues
- pricing rules and valuation restrictions
- tax treatment uncertainty, if drafted poorly

In India, hybrid instruments work best when documentation is conservative and compliant.

Structure Selection Map

Your priority	Best starting structure
Maximum control, brand/IP protection	Wholly owned subsidiary
Need local access, licences, land, relationships	JV with tight governance
Strategic exposure without operating risk	Minority equity + protective rights
Capital protection + predictable returns	Hybrid / structured funding

Control: The Most Misunderstood Element

EU boards often assume shareholding equals control. In India, control is created by documents, not percentages.

You can own 51% and still lose control if:

- reserved matters are weak
- board composition is unfavourable

- quorum rules block decisions
- local partner controls operations informally

Similarly, you can own 30%, and still be protected if:

"In India, control is drafted—not assumed."

- veto rights are well drafted
- governance is balanced
- exit rights are enforceable

Key Governance Tools EU Companies Must Use

- **Reserved matters**: budgets, new debt, related-party transactions, senior hires, capex above threshold, change of business
- **Board composition**: who appoints directors and whether your nominee can actually influence decisions
- **Quorum and voting**: protections against unilateral action and silent deadlock
- **Information rights:** MIS, audited accounts, bank statements, inventory reports, and operating data

Money Movement: Repatriation and Cash Discipline

A major concern for EU investors is simple: can money move out of India safely? The answer is yes, but only if the structure and documentation are correct from day one.

- Dividends, subject to profits and corporate law discipline
- Management fees, where the basis is commercially defensible and documented
- Royalties and licensing fees, with regulatory and tax compliance
- Buyback or sale of shares, with valuation and procedural compliance

The biggest mistakes arise when companies ignore transfer pricing discipline, treat fees as informal cash extraction, or fail to maintain the documentation needed to support money movement.

Tax Exposure: What You Should Plan for

This is not a tax chapter, but the structure must be tax-aware.

Key areas to plan:

- permanent establishment risk (services / sales teams)
- withholding taxes on royalties, fees, interest
- GST implications on services and cross-charges
- capital gains at exit

The right structure does not "avoid tax." It avoids unplanned tax exposure.

Acquisition vs Greenfield: Structural Changes Completely

If you are acquiring an Indian company, you must plan:

- due diligence depth
- legacy liabilities
- warranties and indemnities
- escrow arrangements
- founder retention and non-compete strategy

Acquisitions require stronger documentation than greenfield entries because you inherit history.

If you are building from scratch, you must plan:

- entity setup
- licensing roadmap

- key hires
- vendor and compliance infrastructure

Greenfield is cleaner, but slower.

Greenfield vs Acquisition

Factor	Greenfield (build)	Acquisition (buy)
Speed to market	Slower	Faster
Legacy liabilities	Low	High
Compliance setup	You build	You inherit
Control	High	Negotiated
Cost predictability	Medium	Lower initially, higher risk

Exit Planning: Do This on Day One

"If you cannot describe your exit today, your entry is incomplete."

EU investors often think about exit only after three or four years. In India, exit should be planned on day one because exit depends on shareholder rights, valuation mechanics, regulatory compliance, and actual buyer appetite.

- Strategic sale
- Secondary sale to a financial investor
- Buyback
- IPO, where scale and market conditions support it
- Put/call options, drafted with care

How the FTA Changes Investment Structure Choices

The India–EU FTA does not directly regulate investment structure, but it changes the commercial environment in which structure decisions are made. Companies that previously limited India exposure through minority investments or distributor-led participation may now find that, post-FTA, economics justify a deeper and more direct capital commitment.

As tariffs reduce and service access improves, wholly owned subsidiaries and majority-controlled JVs become more commercially attractive in sectors where pricing, after-sales support, compliance, and customer relationships matter. Post-FTA modelling can also change the expected returns built into hybrid instruments, shareholder loans, and conversion-linked structures. A structure designed on pre-FTA assumptions may no longer fit the business case.

The FTA also raises the stakes on tax, control and exit planning. If India activity scales faster because the economics improve, permanent establishment risk, governance rights and valuation mechanics should all be reviewed against post-FTA reality, rather than historic assumptions.

One further consequence is geopolitical. In a world shaped by sanctions, shipping disruption, and supply-chain stress, local presence in India has greater commercial value. A local subsidiary signals strategic commitment, gives better resilience, and allows a business to respond more effectively than a pure export model managed entirely from Europe.

What Usually Fails in India Investment Structuring

- Overcomplicated instruments that create regulatory or tax confusion
- Weak governance where control is assumed, not documented
- No clear money-movement plan for dividends, fees, royalties, or share sale
- Exit rights that exist only on paper
- Partner mismatch in JVs, especially on time horizon and commercial priorities

These failures are avoidable when structure is built around reality, rather than optimism.

Practical Pointers

- Choose a subsidiary when brand reputation, product liability, stable quality, service control and long-term commitment matter most.
- Choose a JV when the partner brings proven execution capability, licences, land access, or genuine operating leverage, and governance is tight.
- Choose minority investing when you want exposure rather than operations, but only if protective and exit rights are strong.
- Choose debt or hybrid funding when downside protection and structured returns matter more than full operating control.

Chapter Takeaway

The strongest India investors are not always the ones with the biggest budgets. They are the ones with a clean structure, strong governance, disciplined documentation, planned exit, and realistic timelines. India is not hostile to foreign capital. India is unforgiving to weak structures.

Chapter 7

Strategic Acquisition of Distressed Indian Assets

IBC framework, CIRP process, execution roadmap, risk identification, and illustrative case study.

India's Insolvency and Bankruptcy Code, 2016 (**IBC**), has created one of the most structured entry routes available to foreign investors seeking operational assets in India. While most European boards view the India–EU FTA as the main commercial gateway, the Corporate Insolvency Resolution Process (**CIRP**) offers a different kind of opportunity: acquisition of functioning Indian businesses, infrastructure, and industrial platforms through a court-supervised process.

This chapter is written for European corporates, private equity funds, and strategic investors who understand that some of the most valuable India opportunities do not come through conventional market entry. They come through stress, restructuring, and controlled acquisition.

> ***"IBC is not only India's insolvency mechanism. For prepared foreign investors, it is a structured asset acquisition route."***

1. Why CIRP Matters for European Investors

CIRP gives investors access to operating assets that would otherwise be difficult, slow, or expensive to build through greenfield entry. In many cases, the investor is acquiring more than land or machinery. It is acquiring a trained workforce, supplier relationships, customer access, licences, and market presence.

For a European investor, the practical advantages are clear:

- faster entry than greenfield investment
- acquisition pricing is often below replacement cost
- statutory process under National Company Law Tribunal (**NCLT**) oversight
- approved plans bind creditors and reduce legacy uncertainty
- existing operations, registrations, and infrastructure come with the asset

The key commercial point is simple: CIRP can compress years of India entry into a shorter acquisition cycle.

2. Where the Opportunity Usually Appears

CIRP opportunities are most visible in:

- manufacturing and heavy industry
- real estate and infrastructure
- logistics and warehousing
- pharma and life sciences
- hospitality, retail, and consumer businesses

For European investors, this matters because the route is not sector-specific. It is a platform-level opportunity across multiple industries.

3. Why CIRP Can Be Better Than Greenfield

A greenfield investment gives control, but it takes time. Land acquisition, approvals, construction, workforce building, supplier development, and commercial ramp-up can take years.

A CIRP acquisition can provide:

- operating control within a shorter timeframe
- distressed pricing

- existing asset base
- embedded market access
- regulatory and operational head start

That does not make CIRP easier. It makes it different. The advantage comes from speed and existing capacity. The risk comes from diligence, eligibility, and implementation.

4. CIRP in Simple Terms

CIRP begins when a financial creditor, operational creditor, or the company itself approaches the NCLT. Once admitted, a moratorium is declared, and an Interim Resolution Professional (**RP**) takes control. A Committee of Creditors (**CoC**) is formed, a Resolution Professional runs the process, Expression s of Interest are invited, and qualified applicants submit resolution plans.

The key decision-makers are:

- **CoC** – commercial decision-making body
- **RP** – process manager and information gatekeeper
- **NCLT** – adjudicating authority, approving the final plan

For foreign investors, the important point is this: commercial negotiation happens with the CoC, procedural control sits with the RP, and legal finality comes from the NCLT.

5. What Foreign Investors Must Check First

Foreign participation is permitted, but it must comply with:

- FEMA
- FDI policy
- sectoral caps
- RBI reporting requirements
- Section 29A eligibility rules

The most critical early gate is **Section 29A**. A foreign bidder may be disqualified if connected entities fall within the disqualification criteria, including NPA-related exposure. This check must be done before serious participation, not after the bid process has started.

6. Why the SPV Route Usually Works Best

Most European investors should participate through an Indian SPV rather than directly.

The SPV route helps because it:

- ring-fences acquisition exposure
- simplifies FEMA compliance
- creates a clean bidding vehicle
- supports post-acquisition merger or restructuring
- avoids contamination of existing Indian operations

Where sector caps or co-investors are relevant, the SPV also provides structural flexibility.

7. The Practical Execution Roadmap

A workable CIRP acquisition usually follows this sequence:

1. identify target companies
2. review the Information Memorandum
3. assemble legal, tax, regulatory, financial, and technical advisers
4. submit Expression of Interest
5. clear qualification and Section 29A checks
6. conduct focused due diligence
7. prepare and submit the resolution plan
8. negotiate with the CoC

9. obtain CoC approval
10. secure NCLT approval
11. implement, stabilise, and integrate

The process looks linear on paper, but in practice, it is compressed and negotiation-heavy. Investors who are slow on internal approvals or unclear on bid flexibility usually lose momentum.

8. What Usually Goes Wrong

CIRP does not remove risk. It changes the form of risk.

The most common problem areas are:

1. hidden liabilities despite the clean-slate principle
2. pending litigation and contingent claims
3. environmental and statutory exposure
4. operational deterioration during the insolvency period
5. workforce attrition
6. delayed or incomplete regulatory transfers post-approval

NCLT approval is not the end of the process. It is the start of implementation risk.

9. Why CIRP Still Works for Prepared Investors

Despite the risks, CIRP remains powerful for European investors for three reasons.

First, pricing arbitrage.

Banks are focused on recovery, not replacement value. A European bidder with technology, export access, and operational synergies may value the same asset more intelligently than a purely financial bidder and still acquire it at a significant discount.

Second, cleaner control transition.

Unlike conventional M&A, CIRP typically removes legacy promoter influence, giving the acquirer greater freedom to impose governance, reporting, and operating discipline from day one.

Third, judicial backing.

The IBC framework has strong support from Indian courts, especially on the primacy of approved resolution plans and the commercial judgement of the CoC. That gives the process a degree of legal structure not always present in conventional distressed transactions.

10. Do's and Don'ts for European Investors

Do's

1. conduct forensic and legal diligence beyond the Information Memorandum
2. check Section 29A early
3. use experienced India insolvency counsel
4. build bid flexibility before CoC negotiation
5. plan working capital and turnaround funding separately from acquisition price
6. prepare the operational revival plan before bidding

Don'ts

1. do not rely on the IM as a complete disclosure tool
2. do not assume NCLT approval solves all regulatory issues
3. do not overbid without operational clarity
4. do not ignore post-approval implementation timelines
5. do not enter the process without a clear SPV and FEMA structure

Illustrative Outcome: Why CIRP Can Outperform Greenfield

A European manufacturing business evaluating India through greenfield entry may spend years testing the economics without committing. A CIRP acquisition can change that equation by delivering a trained workforce, operating plants, customer access, and market position at a fraction of the replacement cost.

The practical lesson is not that every CIRP case is attractive. It is that, for the right investor, the right case can transform India's entry economics.

What This Chapter Ultimately Means

The IBC was created to resolve distress. In doing so, it also created one of India's most structured acquisition pathways. For European investors, CIRP is not merely a distressed-asset process. It is a serious entry route into India for those who are prepared to act with discipline.

It combines the speed of acquisition with the strategic value of an already-operational platform. But it rewards only those who approach it with the right structure, the right advisory team, and the right implementation plan.

Chapter Takeaway

The common mistake is to treat CIRP as a cheaper version of M&A. It is not. It is a separate acquisition discipline with its own legal gates, negotiation rhythm, and execution risks. Investors who enter it casually usually get trapped in diligence gaps, eligibility issues, or post-approval operational strain.

The investors who succeed are the ones who prepare before they bid, structure before they negotiate, and plan integration before they win.

For prepared European investors, CIRP is not distress at the edge of the market. It is often the most structured way into the market.

SECTION III

HOW DOES TRADE UNDER THE FTA REALLY WORK?

The FTA promises tariff benefits, but execution depends on documentation, classification, and pricing strategy. This section breaks down how tariff reductions influence real commercial decisions and why Rules of Origin and customs processes often determine success more than headline duty cuts. The chapters ahead highlight practical risks at Indian ports and explain how EU exporters can convert policy advantages into predictable trading outcomes. In practice, the difference between a business that captures FTA benefits and one that does not is almost never about the treaty text – it is about the documentation systems, contract provisions, and compliance processes that were designed before the first shipment was made.

Chapter 8

How Do Tariff Reductions Under the FTA Affect Our Pricing?

Phased cuts, exclusions, quotas, landed-cost planning and contract implications.

For most EU companies, the Free Trade Agreement becomes commercially meaningful at one point only: when pricing decisions have to be made.

Everything else - market access, compliance, contracts, and origin - ultimately feeds into one board-level question: Does this make our product more competitive in India, and by how much?

Tariff reductions under the India–EU FTA do not operate like a flat discount. They work through phased cuts, product-specific schedules, exclusions, tariff-rate quotas and compliance conditions. Companies that misunderstand this often overprice, underprice or promise benefits they cannot sustain.

This chapter explains how tariff reductions actually affect pricing, and how EU businesses can convert tariff relief into durable competitiveness, rather than short-term confusion.

> ***"Tariff reduction improves margins only when pricing discipline keeps up."***

1. The First Reality Check: Tariffs Do Not Disappear Overnight

One of the most common misunderstandings is that an FTA means zero duty from day one.

In reality:

1. tariff elimination is often phased
2. sensitive products may be excluded
3. some categories fall under tariff-rate quotas
4. benefits apply only if Rules of Origin are satisfied

This means pricing must be dynamic, not static.

Businesses that price on the assumption of immediate full tariff elimination often face:

"FTA pricing advantage is cumulative, not immediate."

1. denied benefits
2. retrospective duty exposure
3. margin erosion
4. distributor disputes

2. Understanding Phased Tariff Reduction

Under the FTA, tariff reduction usually follows one of four patterns:

1. immediate elimination
2. phased elimination over 3, 5, 7, or 10 years
3. partial reduction with residual duty
4. exclusion from tariff elimination

Each HS code follows its own schedule, which means pricing cannot be decided category-wide in broad terms. It must be tested SKU by SKU.

A typical pattern may look like this:

1. Year 0: limited reduction
2. Year 3: meaningful cumulative reduction
3. Year 5: stronger cost advantage
4. Year 7 to 10: full elimination for eligible products

The commercial implication is simple: pricing advantage grows over time. It rarely appears fully at the start.

3. Exclusions and Quotas: The Hidden Limits

Not all products benefit equally. Every FTA protects some sensitive sectors. Products may be:

1. fully excluded
2. partially excluded
3. subject to residual tariffs
4. covered by tariff-rate quotas

Where tariff-rate quotas apply, the reduced or zero-duty treatment works only up to a defined volume. Beyond that, standard tariffs return. This creates a direct pricing risk. A product that is competitive within quota may become uncompetitive outside it.

This is why quota-sensitive products need volume planning, as well as pricing planning.

"Quota-blind pricing is one of the fastest ways to lose money under an FTA."

4. How Tariff Reduction Actually Affects Price

Tariff reduction affects only one part of the landed cost. It does not remove the rest.

Pricing must still account for:

1. ex-factory price
2. logistics and insurance
3. customs duty after FTA adjustment
4. GST and local taxes
5. distributor margin
6. retail or end-user margin

If customs duty is only a small share of the total landed cost, the actual pricing impact may be modest. If it is material, the effect may be commercially significant. That is why tariff advantage must be measured, not assumed.

5. Where EU Companies Usually Misprice

Three mistakes appear repeatedly.

1. Passing the Full Benefit Immediately

This creates fragile pricing. If the origin is later disputed, quota is exceeded, or tariff reduction is phased more slowly than expected, the company loses flexibility.

2. Locking Long-Term Prices Too Early

Without repricing rights, companies get trapped when tariff schedules, origin outcomes, or landed-cost assumptions shift.

3. Treating All SKUs the Same

Each HS code behaves differently. Blanket discounting across categories usually creates avoidable margin leakage.

"The FTA rewards SKU-level pricing intelligence, not blanket discounts."

6. Pricing Strategy Must Be Reflected in Contracts

Tariff benefits do not become commercially useful unless contracts are built to absorb them.

Pricing clauses in distribution, supply and purchase contracts should address:

1. tariff phase-down
2. quota risk
3. origin qualification risk
4. repricing rights

5. margin allocation

6. denial of benefit after audit

A distribution agreement that locks pricing for two or three years may prevent the exporter from using tariff savings intelligently. Equally, a contract that passes all savings immediately may leave no protection if customs later denies benefit.

These are not minor drafting issues. They determine whether tariff reduction strengthens profitability or creates later disputes.

"Lower tariffs improve competitiveness, not profitability by default."

7. Case Studies: How Pricing Decisions Play Out

Case Study 1: German Industrial Machinery

A German manufacturer selling high-value industrial equipment in India faced a major duty disadvantage against Asian suppliers. Under the FTA, tariffs were phased down over five years.

Pricing strategy:

- partial benefit passed on early
- part of the savings retained as a compliance and audit buffer
- annual repricing aligned with tariff reduction milestones

Outcome:

- gradual market share gain
- stable distributor relationships
- preserved margins

Lesson: Phased tariff reduction should be matched by phased commercial repricing.

Case Study 2: Italian Consumer Goods

An Italian lifestyle brand assumed immediate tariff elimination and priced aggressively from year one.

What went wrong:

- the product faced only partial tariff relief
- actual landed-cost reduction was modest
- distributors resisted a later price correction

Outcome:

- margin erosion
- pricing disputes
- market exit within two years

Lesson: Tariff optimism, without verification, becomes a pricing problem very quickly.

Case Study 3: French Cosmetics

A French cosmetics company received only a moderate tariff benefit, but the brand already had pricing power.

Pricing strategy:

- no direct visible price reduction
- tariff savings used to support marketing and compliance
- premium pricing retained

Outcome:

- stronger brand positioning
- stable profitability
- tariff benefit used strategically, not visibly

Lesson: Tariff benefit does not always need to appear as a price cut; it can support competitiveness indirectly.

8. Cost Competitiveness is Not the Same as Price Reduction

FTA-driven advantage can improve competitiveness in several ways:

1. direct price reduction
2. margin improvement
3. distributor support
4. marketing reinvestment
5. stronger after-sales capability
6. better commercial stability

Reducing price is only one lever. In some sectors, the smarter move is to use tariff relief to improve the commercial proposition without changing visible market pricing immediately.

9. How the FTA Should Change Customer Strategy

Tariff reduction requires a review of customer-facing pricing strategy, not just internal cost models.

In sectors where EU products were previously overpriced in India because of duty burden, even moderate tariff cuts may materially change competitive positioning. This is especially relevant in:

- industrial machinery
- specialised chemicals
- medical devices
- professional equipment
- premium consumer categories

In many of these sectors, the goal is not immediate undercutting. It is to reach pricing parity or workable proximity with lower-cost competitors while preserving the EU supplier's advantage in quality, reliability, service, or regulatory confidence.

A transparent, phased commercial narrative often works better than a one-time price promise. Indian distributors and buyers respond better to pricing that is credible and stable than to aggressive cuts that later need correction.

10. Strategic Pricing Framework for EU Companies

A sound FTA pricing process usually follows five steps:

Step 1: map the tariff schedule SKU by SKU

Step 2: identify exclusions and quota limits

Step 3: calculate duty as a share of landed cost

Step 4: decide how tariff benefit will be allocated

Step 5: build repricing and adjustment rights into contracts

FTA pricing is not a one-time decision. It is a recurring commercial and legal exercise.

Common Mistakes EU Businesses Make at This Stage

1. pricing before tariff schedules are verified
2. assuming all products benefit equally
3. letting sales teams promise unverified savings
4. failing to link pricing with origin compliance
5. using contracts that do not allow repricing
6. ignoring quota and audit risk

These mistakes compound quickly once volumes increase.

Practical Pricing Checklist

Before finalising pricing, confirm:

☐ tariff phase-down schedule verified

☐ product not excluded or partially excluded without adjustment

☐ quota limits understood

☐ origin qualification confirmed

☐ duty share in landed cost calculated

☐ pricing buffers built in

☐ contracts allow repricing and risk allocation

What This Chapter Ultimately Means

The FTA creates a pricing opportunity, but only for businesses that treat tariffs as one input, not a commercial promise.

Companies that price carefully gain:

- stronger competitiveness
- better distributor trust
- more stable margins
- fewer pricing disputes

Those who move too early or promise too much often lose control of both pricing and commercial credibility.

Chapter Takeaway

The most successful EU companies in India do not compete on the lowest price. They compete on the most reliable price, one that survives tariff phase-down, origin review, quota limits, and audit scrutiny.

Pricing strategy and legal structure are inseparable here. Distributor arrangements, tariff-adjustment clauses, landed-cost assumptions, and origin-risk allocation all decide whether FTA margin improvement is captured or lost.

"The FTA can improve your pricing position. Only disciplined execution turns that into a lasting advantage."

Chapter 9

How Do We Prove Our Products Qualify for FTA Benefits?

Rules of Origin explained: what qualifies, what fails, and what documentation is required.

For many EU companies, Rules of Origin (RoO) are the single biggest blind spot under any Free Trade Agreement.

Tariffs attract attention. Market access creates excitement. But, in practice, Rules of Origin decide whether the FTA applies at all.

If you fail on Rules of Origin:

1. tariff benefits are denied
2. duties are demanded retrospectively
3. penalties are imposed
4. future shipments are flagged
5. commercial relationships suffer

"Under an FTA, origin is not where your company is based. It is where value is created."

This chapter explains what Rules of Origin really mean, how to comply in practice, and what happens when companies get it wrong.

Why Rules of Origin Exist

Rules of Origin exist to answer one question:

Is this product genuinely made in the FTA partner country, or is it only passing through?

Customs authorities use Rules of Origin to:

- prevent third-country goods from misusing FTA benefits
- protect domestic industries
- ensure fair trade

From the regulator's perspective, Rules of Origin are the backbone of the FTA.

From the business perspective, they are the price of admission.

The Biggest Misunderstanding EU Companies Have

Many EU exporters assume:

- "We are an EU company, so our products qualify."
- "Final assembly in the EU is enough."
- "Our supplier handles origin."

All three assumptions are risky.

Origin is about the product, not the passport of the company.

The Three Core Ways a Product Qualifies as 'Originating'

Most FTAs, including the India–EU FTA, recognise three main methods.

1. Wholly Obtained Products

These are products that are entirely produced in one country, such as:

- agricultural produce
- minerals extracted locally
- animals born and raised locally

Example:

Italian olive oil made entirely from olives grown, pressed and bottled in Italy.

This category is simple—but limited.

2. Substantial Transformation

This is the most common route for manufactured goods.

A product qualifies if it undergoes significant manufacturing or processing that changes its nature.

The FTA defines this through:

- change in tariff classification (CTC), or
- specific processing rules

3. Value-Addition Thresholds

Many products qualify only if a minimum percentage of value is added within the EU.

For example:

- at least 40% EU value content, or
- non-originating materials must not exceed a defined percentage

"Rules of Origin reward real manufacturing, not clever routing."

This requires precise cost and sourcing calculations.

Why EU Supply Chains Are More Exposed

EU companies typically operate complex supply chains.

- components sourced from Asia
- intermediate processing in multiple EU countries
- final assembly in one EU member state

This is efficient, but risky for origin compliance.

A product may be:

- legally manufactured
- commercially sound
- technically advanced

and still fail Rules of Origin.

Practical Product Case Studies

Case Study 1: German Industrial Machinery (Qualifies)

Product: Industrial packaging machine

Supply chain:

- Steel and motors sourced partly from the EU and partly from non-EU
- Core engineering, assembly and testing done in Germany
- EU value addition exceeds threshold

Outcome: Product qualifies as EU originating.

Why: Substantial transformation and sufficient value addition occur in Germany.

Case Study 2: Italian Fashion Garments (Does NOT Qualify)

Product: Premium jackets

Supply chain:

- Fabric sourced from a non-EU country
- Stitching and finishing done in Italy
- Value addition in Italy is low

Outcome: Fails Rules of Origin.

Why: Simple stitching is not considered substantial transformation, and EU value content is insufficient.

Commercial impact: FTA tariff benefit denied at Indian customs.

Case Study 3: French Cosmetics (Conditional Qualification)

Product: Skincare cream

Supply chain:

- Active ingredients imported
- Formulation, blending, testing, packaging in France

Outcome: Qualification depends on:

- whether formulation is recognised as a substantial transformation
- whether value thresholds are met

Lesson: Cosmetics often sit in grey zones and require advanced origin analysis.

Case Study 4: Dutch Electronics Assembly (Fails)

Product: Consumer electronics device

Supply chain:

- Components imported from Asia
- Assembly and packaging in the Netherlands

Outcome: Does not qualify.

Why: Assembly and packaging alone do not change tariff classification.

Certificates of Origin: Where Execution Often Breaks

Even if a product qualifies, benefits are lost if documentation fails.

To claim FTA benefits, exporters must provide:

- a valid Certificate of Origin (CoO)
- issued by an authorised body
- matching shipment details exactly

Common failures include:

- wrong product description
- mismatched HS codes
- expired or incorrect supplier declarations
- clerical errors

Customs authorities do not "fix" CoOs. They reject them.

Real Consequence Cases (What Actually Happens When RoO is Ignored)

Consequence Case 1: Retrospective Duty Demand

An EU exporter claimed FTA benefits for multiple shipments over two years.

During a post-clearance audit, Indian customs questioned origin documentation.

Result:

- preferential duty withdrawn retrospectively
- full customs duty demanded
- penalties imposed
- future shipments flagged for inspection

The commercial damage was greater than the duty amount.

Consequence Case 2: Distributor Relationship Breakdown

An EU manufacturer promised FTA pricing to an Indian distributor.

Later, customs denied origin benefits.

Result:

- distributor refused to absorb additional duty
- pricing disputes escalated

- relationship terminated
- market reputation damaged

Consequence Case 3: Criminal Exposure (Extreme Cases)

In cases of repeated or intentional misdeclaration, customs authorities may:

"The cost of getting Rules of Origin wrong is rarely limited to customs duty."

- initiate investigations
- impose severe penalties
- suspend import privileges

While rare, the risk exists—especially where patterns suggest misuse.

Who Bears the Risk: Exporter or Importer?

Legally:

- the importer of record bears primary liability

Practically:

- brand owners and exporters are investigated
- distributors push liability back contractually
- reputational damage sits with the exporter

EU companies must not assume distributors "**carry the risk**."

How Smart Companies Manage RoO Risk

Successful exporters do the following:

1. Pre-classification and origin testing
2. Written origin calculations for each SKU
3. Supplier declarations updated regularly
4. Internal audit before first shipment

5. Contract clauses allocating RoO risk

Rules of Origin must be treated as a system, not a document.

Pricing Strategy and RoO Risk

Never:

- guarantee FTA pricing, contractually
- build margins, assuming permanent tariff benefit
- lock long-term prices without origin buffers

Best practice:

- price conservatively
- disclose RoO dependency clearly
- include adjustment clauses

> ***"Never sell today on an origin assumption you cannot defend tomorrow."***

Rules of Origin and Services: A Common Confusion

Rules of Origin apply only to goods, not services.

However, confusion arises when:

- software is embedded in hardware
- bundled supply includes goods + services
- after-sales services affect valuation

Clear separation in contracts and invoices is essential.

Post-Clearance Audits: The Long Tail Risk

Indian customs increasingly rely on:

- post-clearance audits
- data analytics
- historical pattern reviews

Audits can look back several years.

If origin documentation cannot be produced later, benefits can be reversed, even if goods cleared earlier.

Practical Checklist (Before Claiming FTA Benefits)

Before claiming RoO benefits, confirm:

1. Product-wise origin analysis completed
2. Value-addition calculation documented
3. Supplier declarations current and verifiable
4. HS classification stable and defensible
5. Certificate of Origin process tested
6. Distributor contracts allocate RoO risk

If any answer is "**no,**" pause.

Typical RoO Failure Points

Stage	Common failure
Product design	No origin analysis
Sourcing	Excess non-origin inputs
Documentation	Incorrect CoO
Pricing	Assumed tariff benefit
Audits	Missing historical records

What Goes Wrong When Origin is Assumed Rather Than Proved

The most serious Rules of Origin failures are usually not caused by deliberate misrepresentation. They are caused by assumption. An exporter assumes that EU manufacturing automatically means EU origin. A compliance team assumes that earlier clearance means the documentation is sound. A logistics team assumes that the customs broker has checked origin properly. None of these assumptions replaces actual origin analysis, and each can create significant legal and commercial exposure in India.

When origin is assumed and later challenged, the consequences escalate quickly. The first is denial of FTA duty treatment and assessment of full customs duty on the shipments concerned. The second is retrospective exposure: post-clearance audits may reopen prior shipments and raise duty, interest and penalty demands across a wider period. The third is operational disruption – management time is diverted, distributor confidence weakens, and customers begin to question the reliability of the exporter's compliance discipline.

The practical safeguard is early origin verification. Before claiming FTA benefits, EU exporters should carry out product-level origin analysis, map supplier inputs and value addition, obtain written supplier declarations, and build review procedures that are repeated whenever the supply-chain changes. Origin compliance is not a one-time exercise. What qualified last year may fail this year if sourcing changes.

Chapter Takeaway

The pattern in origin disputes is consistent: most arise not from dishonesty, but from assumptions checked too late, a supplier assumed to qualify, a threshold assumed to be met, a certificate assumed to match the shipment. In practice, origin problems are usually documentation problems. The manufacturing may be genuine; the paperwork is weak. The remedy is systematic and must be in place before the first FTA-benefit shipment, not after the first audit notice.

Customs authorities do not negotiate origin; they verify it.

Chapter 10

What Can Go Wrong at Indian Customs?

Classification, valuation, post-clearance audits, penalties, and logistics disruption risk.

For most EU companies, customs is seen as a logistics function, something that happens after the sale, handled by freight forwarders, customs brokers, or distributors.

In India, this assumption is dangerous.

Indian customs are not only a tax collection mechanism. It is a regulatory enforcement system, backed by data analytics, post-clearance audits, and wide powers under law. Many EU companies discover customs risk only after shipments are delayed, duties are reassessed, or notices are issued years later.

> ***"In India, customs risk is legal risk disguised as logistics."***

This chapter explains where customs problems actually arise, how Indian authorities think, and how EU businesses can protect themselves without becoming overly conservative.

Why Indian Customs Feel Unforgiving to Foreign Companies

Indian customs operate under a framework that prioritises:

- revenue protection
- misuse prevention (especially under FTAs)
- Audit-based enforcement

Over the last decade, Indian customs have shifted from:

- physical inspection → risk-based assessment
- port-level checks → post-clearance audits
- shipment-by-shipment review → pattern analysis

This means:

- Your first shipment may clear smoothly
- Your 10th shipment may be questioned
- Your 100th shipment may trigger an audit

Customs compliance is judged over time, not at the border alone.

The Five Core Risk Areas at Indian Customs

Almost every serious customs issue faced by EU companies falls into one of these five buckets:

1. Classification errors
2. Valuation disputes
3. Rules of Origin misuse (intentional or accidental)
4. Post-clearance audits and retrospective demands
5. Penalties and prosecution risk

Each is examined below in detail.

1. Classification: The Silent Profit Killer

What Classification Means

Customs classification is the process of assigning the correct HS code to imported goods. This code determines:

- applicable customs duty
- eligibility under FTAs
- regulatory requirements

- licensing obligations

A wrong classification can:

- increase duty
- invalidate FTA benefits
- attract penalties

Why Classification Goes Wrong

EU companies often assume:

- HS codes are uniform globally
- EU classification is accepted automatically
- Customs brokers "will handle it"

In reality:

- HS interpretation can differ, country to country
- Indian customs apply Indian tariff schedules and explanatory notes
- Brokers rely on information you provide

Even minor description differences can change classification.

Real-World Example

An EU machinery exporter classified equipment under a general machinery heading. Indian customs reclassified it under a specific industrial machinery category, with higher duty and additional compliance.

"At customs, one word in a product description can change your tax outcome."

Result:

- duty differential demanded
- penalties imposed
- future shipments flagged

2. Valuation: Where Most Serious Disputes Begin

What Customs Valuation Covers

Indian customs valuation is governed by the principle of transaction value, but with strict rules.

Customs examines whether:

- the declared price reflects actual consideration
- parties are related
- additional costs should be added

These additions can include:

- royalties and licence fees
- commissions
- tooling or design costs
- assists provided free of cost

Why EU Companies Get Valuation Wrong

Common reasons:

- transfer pricing logic is confused with customs valuation
- royalties are not disclosed
- management fees are ignored
- discounts are not properly documented

Customs do not accept "group pricing" unless justified clearly.

Real-World Example

An EU parent charged royalty separately from the product price. Customs held that the royalty was a condition of sale and added it to the assessable value.

Result:

- higher duty assessed
- retrospective demands
- extended audit scrutiny

"Customs valuation looks at economic reality, not accounting labels."

3. Rules of Origin: The Most Sensitive Area Post-FTA

Rules of Origin (RoO) issues deserve special mention because they now trigger heightened scrutiny under FTAs.

Customs authorities closely examine:

- whether goods truly originate in the EU
- supplier declarations
- value-addition calculations

Even technical or clerical mistakes can result in:

- denial of preferential duty
- retrospective duty demand
- penalties

RoO failures are often treated more seriously than simple classification errors because they involve preferential treatment misuse.

4. Post-Clearance Audits: Where Past Mistakes Resurface

Indian customs increasingly rely on post-clearance audits (PCA).

What Audits Cover

Audits may examine:

- classification history
- valuation methodology
- related-party transactions

- origin claims
- documentation consistency

Audits can go back five years or more.

Why Audits Hurt EU Companies

EU companies often:

- do not retain historical documents
- rely on distributors who lack records
- change brokers without data continuity

Customs is not sympathetic to "records no longer available."

"In Indian customs audits, yesterday's paperwork decides today's liability."

5. Penalties and Prosecution: When Issues Escalate

Indian customs law provides for:

- monetary penalties
- confiscation of goods
- interest on duty
- prosecution in extreme cases

While prosecution is rare for genuine mistakes, penalties are common when:

- misdeclaration is repeated
- explanations are inconsistent
- documentation appears careless

The law distinguishes between:

- error
- negligence
- wilful misstatement

The burden often falls on the importer to prove absence of intent.

Distributors and Importers: Who Actually Bears the Risk?

Legally: the importer of record is liable

Practically:

- authorities investigate the brand owner
- distributors pass liability contractually
- reputational risk stays with exporter

EU companies must treat distributor imports as their own compliance exposure.

Dispute Resolution: What Happens If You Challenge Customs

> ***"Most customs disputes are won or lost before the first notice is issued."***

Disputes typically follow this path:

1. Show cause notice
2. Adjudication by customs authority
3. Appeal to appellate tribunal
4. Further appeal to courts

This process:

- takes time
- requires documentation discipline
- consumes management attention

Many disputes arise because issues were not addressed early.

Strategic Reality: Conservative Today or Defensive Tomorrow

EU companies must decide:

- whether to take aggressive positions upfront
- or adopt conservative, defensible approaches

In India, conservative positions usually:

- reduce long-term cost
- improve predictability
- limit audit exposure

Aggressive positions may boost short-term margins, but often lead to:

- audits
- disputes
- retrospective liabilities

Five Customs Disciplines EU Businesses Must Get Right Before Importing into India

1. Classification must be settled before the first shipment

The product should be classified under the Indian Customs Tariff Act based on its actual technical character, not a commercial label or legacy code used elsewhere. The tariff code should remain consistent across invoices, Bills of Entry, and certificates of origin. For higher-risk or borderline products, an advance ruling should be considered, and broker instructions should be documented clearly.

2. Valuation must reflect the full commercial reality

Import value should capture all relevant considerations, including related-party pricing issues, royalties, licence fees, and structured discounts where applicable. Customs valuation and transfer pricing should not sit in conflict. The importer must be able to explain why the declared value is complete, commercial, and defensible.

3. Rules of Origin must be proved, not assumed

Origin analysis should be carried out SKU by SKU. Supplier declarations must be current, value-addition calculations should be retained in writing, and the certificate of origin must be checked for accuracy before shipment. Contracts should also allocate origin risk clearly so that disputes over denied FTA benefits do not become commercial disputes between the parties.

4. Audit readiness must exist from day one

Indian customs compliance is not complete once the goods are cleared. Bills of Entry, invoices, origin files, valuation working papers, broker correspondence, and internal SOPs should be maintained in an organised form for the audit period. If the business uses an Indian distributor or importer, the agreement should also preserve visibility and audit rights over customs compliance.

5. Penalty exposure usually comes from patterns, not one-off errors.

Repeated misclassification, inconsistent declarations, incomplete supporting records, overdependence on brokers, and delayed responses to customs notices create avoidable penalty risk. A customs issue is rarely just a filing problem; it often becomes a control problem.

Customs Risk vs Company Preparedness

Preparedness level	Likely outcome
Ad-hoc compliance	Delays, penalties
Partial controls	Inconsistent audits
Structured review	Predictable clearance
Audit-ready systems	Low dispute risk

What This Chapter Ultimately Means

Indian customs are not anti-business. It is process-driven and documentation-driven. That distinction matters. Customs disputes in India are rarely just technical disputes about tariff headings, declared value, or origin paperwork. They become commercial problems very quickly.

When goods are delayed, detained, or reassessed, the effects move beyond duty exposure. Working capital gets blocked, delivery timelines slip, distributors and customers lose confidence. Production, service commitments, and supply planning come under pressure. In sectors dependent on timely imports, even a short customs disruption can create consequences far greater than the immediate duty demand or penalty.

This is why customs compliance must be treated as a legal and business control function, not merely a logistics activity. EU companies that settle classification early, validate valuation properly, verify origin carefully, and prepare for audit before it happens face far fewer disruptions. They do not avoid risk because their products are simpler. They avoid risk because their documentation, ownership, and internal discipline are stronger.

Chapter Takeaway

The pattern in cross-border customs disputes is consistent: most are not fraud cases. They are discipline failures. Classification is delegated without verification. Valuation is declared without proper customs support. Origin is claimed without documents that can survive audit. Indian customs enforce what is declared, not what was intended.

Freight volatility and route disruption make this even more important. Longer transit times can affect certificate validity, delay clearance, and increase landed cost through higher CIF-based duty exposure. FTA benefits improve the economics of India trade, but they do not reduce the need for customs discipline.

The businesses that perform best in India are not the ones that treat customs as paperwork completed after shipment. They are the ones that treat it as part of transaction planning, contract discipline, and business continuity from the start.

SECTION IV

WHAT COMPLIANCE AND STANDARDS MUST WE MEET?

Regulatory compliance in India is sector-driven and often misunderstood by first-time entrants. This section introduces the standards, certifications, and non-tariff barriers that shape timelines and operational planning. Rather than viewing compliance as a final step, the chapters ahead show how early alignment with regulators, documentation culture, and product approvals can prevent costly delays and reduce friction during market entry. The FTA opens the tariff gate. Compliance opens the market gate. Both must be managed, and the compliance gate does not open simply because the tariff gate has.

Chapter 11

What Product Standards and Certifications Are Required in India?

BIS, CDSCO, FSSAI, sector approvals, and why delays outlast FTA market access.

For many EU companies, product compliance is the first serious reality check after deciding to enter India.

A common assumption is this:

"If our product meets EU standards, India should accept it."

That assumption is incorrect.

India does not automatically recognise EU certifications. India has its **own product standards regime**, enforced by **sector-specific regulators**, with distinct testing, documentation, and approval requirements.

This chapter explains:

- which certifications are mandatory
- which regulators matter for which products
- where EU companies lose time and money
- how to plan approvals without stalling business

"In India, market access depends as much on certification as on price."

The Big Picture: India's Product Compliance Framework

India regulates products through **multiple regulators**, not a single authority. Each regulator governs a specific product category and applies **mandatory standards**, not voluntary guidelines.

The most important point for EU businesses to understand is this:

Certification in India is product-specific, not company-specific.

Even a globally reputed EU manufacturer must comply, product by product.

The Four Regulators EU Companies Encounter Most Often

Most EU companies entering India deal with one or more of the following:

1. **Bureau of Indian Standards (BIS)** – industrial and consumer products
2. **Central Drugs Standard Control Organization (CDSCO)** – pharmaceuticals and medical devices
3. **Food Safety and Standards Authority of India (FSSAI)** – food, beverages, nutraceuticals
4. **Sector Regulators** (telecom, energy, automotive, chemicals, etc.)

"India does not have one approval system. It has many, and they do not talk to each other."

Each operates independently. Clearing one does not clear the others.

1. BIS Certification – The Most Common Entry Barrier

What BIS Regulates

BIS governs standards for:

- industrial machinery
- electrical and electronic products

- construction materials
- consumer durables
- safety-critical equipment

Many products **cannot be imported or sold** in India without BIS certification.

Mandatory vs Voluntary BIS Standards

This distinction is critical.

- **Mandatory certification** → product cannot enter the market without approval
- **Voluntary standards** → compliance optional, but often expected by customers

EU companies frequently misjudge this distinction.

How BIS Certification Actually Works

For foreign manufacturers, BIS typically requires:

- product testing in BIS-recognised laboratories
- factory inspection (often overseas)
- ongoing compliance and surveillance

This is not a one-time exercise. Certification must be **maintained**, not just obtained.

Where EU Companies Face Delays with BIS

Delays usually occur due to:

- incorrect product classification
- incomplete technical documentation
- misunderstanding Indian standards vs EU norms
- factory audit scheduling issues
- slow response to clarification queries

"BIS does not judge how advanced your product is. It judges, whether it fits Indian standards."

Reality check:

Even technically superior products fail BIS scrutiny if documentation is weak.

2. CDSCO – Pharma and Medical Devices

What CDSCO Regulates

CDSCO governs:

- pharmaceuticals
- medical devices
- diagnostics
- certain cosmetics

This is one of the most tightly regulated entry paths.

Key CDSCO Realities for EU Companies

- EU approvals do **not** substitute Indian approvals
- Clinical data requirements may differ
- Medical devices are increasingly regulated in phases
- Import licences are product-specific

Even minor classification differences can shift a product into a higher regulatory category.

Where CDSCO Delays Happen

Common reasons include:

- incomplete clinical documentation
- mismatch between EU and Indian product classification
- changing regulatory scope (especially for medical devices)
- reliance on local agents, without regulatory depth

CDSCO timelines improve significantly when filings are **conservative and complete**.

3. FSSAI – Food, Beverage, and Nutraceuticals

What FSSAI Covers

FSSAI regulates:

- packaged food
- beverages
- supplements
- health foods
- ingredients and additives

For EU food companies, FSSAI compliance is often the **biggest surprise**.

Why EU Food Products Face Issues in India

Common pain points:

- ingredients permitted in the EU, but restricted in India
- labelling rules that differ significantly
- claims and marketing restrictions
- shelf-life and packaging norms

"In India, what you say on the label matters as much as what is inside the product."

FSSAI is strict on **consumer protection**, not brand reputation.

4. Sector-Specific Approvals

Beyond BIS, CDSCO and FSSAI, EU companies may face sector regulators such as:

- telecom equipment authorities
- energy and power regulators
- automotive homologation bodies
- chemical safety regulators

These approvals are often **parallel**, not sequential.

Failing to plan for them leads to:

- port delays
- storage costs
- expired documentation

Why Certification Delays Really Happen

Certification delays are rarely caused by bureaucracy alone. They usually arise because India-specific requirements were underestimated, documentation remained EU-centric, timelines were unrealistic, or compliance was handed to distributors without sufficient control. India's regulators are process-driven. They reward preparation, not pressure.

How Smart EU Companies Plan Certification

Businesses that manage certification well do four things early: they identify product-specific regulatory requirements, confirm whether compliance is mandatory or voluntary, build certification timelines into the launch plan, and retain control over filings even when local agents are used. Certification is not an administrative afterthought. It is part of market-entry design.

What This Chapter Ultimately Means

Product standards are not a technical inconvenience. They are a market-access gate. The India–EU FTA may reduce tariff friction, but it does not reduce or bypass India's certification requirements. In regulated sectors, the ability to sell in India still depends on whether the product is approved, tested, labelled, and documented in a manner Indian regulators accept.

EU companies that integrate certification into entry planning move faster in real terms. Those that treat certification as a post-entry task often lose time, money and credibility.

Chapter Takeaway

A common mistake among EU companies is to assume that improved FTA market access means easier regulatory access. It does not. BIS, CDSCO, FSSAI, and other sectoral approvals continue on their own timelines and must be addressed independently. Where mutual recognition or regulatory cooperation becomes available, it should be treated as a benefit to verify, not an assumption to rely upon.

India does not block products arbitrarily. It stops products that arrive unprepared. The companies that enter smoothly are not the ones with the strongest commercial intent, but the ones that align certification strategy with market-entry strategy from the beginning.

Chapter 12

What Non-Tariff Barriers Will We Face in Practice?

Licensing, inspections, documentation culture, and compliance friction at scale.

When EU companies think about market access under the India–EU FTA, attention naturally goes to tariffs. Once tariffs are addressed, many assume the hard part is over.

In reality, tariffs are only the visible barrier.

The real friction often comes from **non-tariff barriers (NTBs)**—procedural, regulatory, and operational requirements that sit outside customs duty but directly affect time, cost and predictability.

Non-tariff barriers do not usually block entry outright. Instead, they **slow you down**, **increase operating costs**, and **test internal discipline**. Companies that are unprepared experience India as "difficult." Companies that plan for NTBs experience India as "procedural but manageable."

> ***"In India, trade rarely stops at tariffs. It slows down the procedures."***

This chapter explains what non-tariff barriers look like on the ground and how EU businesses can manage them without losing momentum.

Understanding Non-Tariff Barriers in the Indian Context

Non-tariff barriers are not informal obstacles. They are legal, procedural, and administrative requirements that exist alongside tariff rules.

Typical NTBs include:

- licences and registrations
- inspections and audits
- documentation standards
- testing and sampling
- compliance reporting
- procedural delays

Most of these are **lawful and rule-based**. The challenge is that they are:

- fragmented across authorities
- applied with varying intensity
- heavily documentation-driven

The India–EU FTA does not eliminate NTBs. At best, it improves transparency over time. In the short to medium term, **NTBs remain the main execution challenge**.

The First Reality Check: NTBs Are Sector-Specific

There is no single list of non-tariff barriers that applies to all products or services.

For example:

- a machinery exporter faces inspections and safety documentation
- a food exporter faces ingredient approvals and labelling scrutiny
- a medical device company faces audits and post-market surveillance
- a services company faces registrations, tax compliance, and reporting

"Non-tariff barriers do not block markets. They test preparation."

EU companies struggle when they assume NTBs are uniform.

They are not.

Licensing: Where Entry Often Slows First

Why Licensing Feels Frictional

Licences in India are usually:

- activity-specific
- location-specific
- product-specific

A company may be legally incorporated and still unable to operate fully because:

- a manufacturing licence is pending
- an import licence is product-linked
- a state-level registration is incomplete

EU companies often underestimate how many parallel licences are needed.

Common Licensing Pain Points

Licensing delays usually arise due to:

- incorrect activity classification
- mismatch between licence scope and actual operations
- lack of local experience in filings
- dependence on third parties without oversight

Licences are rarely denied arbitrarily. They are delayed because applications are incomplete or inconsistent.

Inspections: The Most Misunderstood Barrier

What Inspections Are

Inspections are not accusations.

They are a routine compliance tool.

Inspections may cover:

- factories
- warehouses
- imported consignments
- records and registers

For EU companies, inspections feel intrusive because:

- they are more frequent than in many EU jurisdictions
- they focus heavily on paperwork
- inspectors expect immediate access to records

Why Inspections Cause Stress for EU Companies

Inspections become problematic when:

- documentation is not readily available
- records are inconsistent across departments
- responsibility is unclear (HQ vs India team vs distributor)

In many cases, inspectors are less concerned with minor non-compliance and more concerned with how seriously compliance is treated.

"In India, inspections reward readiness, not perfection."

Documentation Culture: The Core NTB

If there is one theme that runs through all non-tariff barriers in India, it is this:

Documentation matters more than explanations.

Indian regulators operate in a system where:

- written records prevail over oral clarifications
- consistency across documents is critical
- historical records are frequently reviewed

EU companies often rely on:

- informal explanations
- business logic
- after-the-fact clarifications

These approaches rarely work in India.

What "Good Documentation" Means in India

Good documentation is:

- complete
- consistent
- contemporaneous
- retrievable

It is not enough that records exist somewhere.

They must be **available on demand** and **aligned across filings**.

Compliance Reporting: Ongoing, Not One-Time

Many EU companies approach compliance as a one-time entry task. In India, compliance is **continuous**.

Examples:

- periodic filings
- renewals of licences
- updates on product changes
- reporting of imports, sales, and manufacturing

Missing a routine filing can trigger:

- notices
- inspections

- suspension of benefits
- penalties

None of these is dramatic on its own, but they compound.

"India does not punish entry mistakes as much as it punishes neglect."

State-Level Variations: One Country, Many Practices

India operates under a federal system.

This means:

- central laws apply nationwide
- states control many operational approvals

As a result:

- timelines vary by state
- enforcement intensity differs
- interpretation can change

EU companies that expand into multiple Indian states often experience:

- uneven compliance experiences
- duplicated paperwork
- different inspection cultures

This is not inconsistency, it is a federal **reality**.

The Role of Intermediaries: Helpful but Risky

EU companies often rely on:

- distributors
- customs brokers

- consultants
- local agents

While intermediaries are necessary, they also create risk when:

- responsibility is outsourced without oversight
- filings are made without HQ visibility
- shortcuts are taken to "save time"

Regulators do not distinguish between:

- mistakes made by your agent
- mistakes made by you

Liability usually travels back to the brand owner.

Why NTBs Feel Worse During Scale-Up

Many EU companies report that:

- initial entry was smooth
- problems arose later

This is because NTBs intensify when:

- volumes increase
- geographic footprint expands
- product range grows
- scrutiny increases

The FTA accelerates scale.

Scale exposes weaknesses.

"Non-tariff barriers rarely stop pilots. They challenge the scale."

Real-World Examples of NTB Friction

Example 1: Licensing Lag

An EU manufacturer obtained central approvals, but delayed state-level licences. Operations started, but inspections flagged missing local permissions.

Impact: Temporary shutdown, loss of production days, reputational damage.

Lesson: Central approval does not replace local compliance.

Example 2: Documentation Gap

A distributor handled imports for years. During an inspection, historical documents were missing.

Impact: Extended audit, penalties, and strained distributor relationship.

Lesson: Outsourced compliance still needs internal control.

Example 3: Inspection Shock

A food importer faced a surprise warehouse inspection. Records were available, but not organised.

Impact: Delays, corrective actions, follow-up inspections.

Lesson: Availability of documents matters as much as their existence.

Are NTBs a Form of Protectionism?

From a business perspective, NTBs feel restrictive. From a regulatory perspective, they are:

- consumer protection tools
- safety enforcement mechanisms
- revenue safeguards

Most NTBs apply equally to domestic and foreign companies.

The issue is not discrimination.

It is **procedural intensity**.

How Smart EU Companies Reduce NTB Friction

Companies that manage NTBs well do five things consistently:

1. **Map NTBs early** – before entry, not after
2. **Build compliance into operations** – not as an add-on

3. **Retain visibility** – even when outsourcing
4. **Train local teams** – compliance culture matters
5. **Expect inspections** – and prepare for them

They treat NTBs as **operational costs**, not surprises.

Table: Non-Tariff Barrier vs Business Impact

NTB type	If unmanaged	If planned
Licensing	Delays, shutdowns	Predictable timelines
Inspections	Disruption	Routine compliance
Documentation	Penalties	Smooth audits
Reporting	Notices	Low visibility
State variation	Confusion	Scalable playbook

What This Chapter Ultimately Means

Non-tariff barriers are not walls. They are speed bumps. Companies that hit them unprepared experience delay, frustration and cost. Companies that plan for them maintain momentum.

The India–EU FTA improves market access, non-discrimination and regulatory transparency. It does not remove the licensing, certification and documentation requirements that govern actual business operations in India. Treaty access and local compliance operate at different levels. Confusing one for the other is one of the most common entry errors EU businesses make.

A product may benefit from reduced duty under the FTA and still remain commercially blocked in India. In food and beverage, FSSAI approvals must be in place before products can move from port to shelf. In pharmaceuticals, CDSCO timelines continue independently of FTA economics. In electronics and consumer goods, BIS certification may still determine whether import and sale are legally possible at all.

Chapter Takeaway

Most foreign companies do not struggle in India because of hostile regulation. They struggle because the process is underestimated. India rewards companies that respect procedure and plan for friction.

Under the India–EU FTA, trade will grow. With growth comes scrutiny. Businesses that treat non-tariff barriers as part of an entry strategy, not as an inconvenience, scale faster and with fewer surprises.

SECTION V

HOW DO WE OPERATE SAFELY IN INDIA?

This section turns from market entry to operational discipline. Once an EU business begins trading, contracting, hiring, and investing in India, the real legal risk shifts from entry approvals to execution quality. This section examines how Indian contracts work in practice, which standard EU clauses need redrafting for Indian realities, and how control rights must be built into governance from the start. The objective is not only to enter India, but to operate there with enforceability, visibility, and protection. In India, safety in business operations comes less from broad legal rights and more from how precisely those rights are documented, structured, and preserved.

Chapter 13

Will Our Contracts Be Enforced in India?

Courts, arbitration, enforcement reality and how to structure Indian legal outcomes.

A fair concern for any EU company entering India is simple:

"If a dispute occurs, will the contract actually be enforced?"

The honest answer is: Yes, contracts are enforceable in India, and the system has become meaningfully more arbitration-friendly and enforcement-oriented over the last decade. But enforcement is not "automatic." India rewards parties who draft clearly, choose the right dispute mechanism, and follow procedure cleanly.

This chapter gives you (i) a practical enforcement picture, (ii) a layman-friendly arbitration procedure, and (iii) real Supreme Court guidance showing a generally pro-arbitration, pro-enforcement direction.

The Practical Enforcement Picture in India

- What works well: Arbitration is now the default "serious" route for commercial disputes because courts have repeatedly emphasised minimal interference and respect for arbitral awards.
- Foreign awards are increasingly enforced, and refusal is meant to be rare, with a high threshold. The Supreme Court has explicitly stressed that Indian courts should enforce foreign

awards unless there is a clear violation of the narrow refusal grounds.

- Interim protection is available (injunctions, asset protection, status quo orders) through courts and tribunals, crucial when a party fears money being moved or assets being diverted.
- Commercial courts and specialised benches in many states have improved discipline and speed for commercial matters (not perfect, but better than a decade ago).

What still needs realistic planning

- Litigation timelines can be long, especially in ordinary civil courts.
- Procedure matters a lot. A strong legal position can still suffer if documents, notices, and pleadings are sloppy.
- Execution (recovery) can take time if the losing party resists and assets are hard to trace, so contracts must include security levers.

Bottom line:

If enforcement is your priority, structure contracts for arbitration + interim relief + security + clean evidence.

Courts vs Arbitration: Which is Better for an EU Company?

Courts

Courts work when:

- the dispute is small and local
- you need statutory remedies (some IP, certain regulatory matters)
- there is no arbitration clause, and renegotiating one is not practical

But for cross-border trade and investment disputes, courts are usually not the best first choice.

Arbitration

Arbitration is preferred because:

- parties can choose arbitrators with industry expertise
- proceedings are private
- enforcement is structured
- the scope for challenging an award is limited by statute

India's Supreme Court has consistently reaffirmed that a Section 34 court has supervisory, not appellate powers, meaning it should not re-hear the case like an appeal.

What Happens After the Award in India

Domestic arbitration seated in India

If the losing party challenges the award, they usually file under Section 34 (set-aside).

Key point: Section 34 is not an "appeal on merits." Courts are not supposed to re-evaluate facts and re-run the trial. The Supreme Court reaffirmed the limited nature of Section 34 review and the need for courts to be careful while interfering with arbitral reasoning.

Can courts "fix" or "modify" an award?

This is where many businesspeople get confused.

A 2025 Supreme Court decision (reference judgement) reaffirmed that courts generally do not have the power to modify arbitral awards under Section 34; their power is primarily to set aside on limited grounds, with narrow exceptions for clerical/computation-type errors and severance principles.

Why this is positive: It strengthens finality. The award is less likely to become a "never-ending" matter in court.

Foreign awards

Foreign awards are enforced in India under the "foreign award" framework. The refusal grounds are narrow.

A strong illustration is the Supreme Court's 2024 decision in *Avitel Post Studioz Ltd. v HSBC PI Holdings (Mauritius) Ltd.*, where the Court emphasised:

- interference with a foreign award is exceptional
- Section 48 refusal is a high threshold
- courts should discourage unmerited resistance to enforcement and push early enforcement

Takeaway: If you choose a credible institution and seat, and run a clean arbitration, enforcement in India is realistically achievable.

Interim Protection: The "Must-Have" in an Indian Enforcement Strategy

Even if you have the best clause, a practical risk remains:

What if the counterparty diverts assets while the dispute is pending?

India provides interim protection tools that can be used intelligently:

- court interim measures (typically under Section 9, for India-seated arbitration—depending on drafting and context)
- tribunal interim measures (Section 17-type powers, with court-backed enforceability)

A major positive development was the Supreme Court's 2021 decision in *Amazon.com NV Investment Holdings LLC v Future Retail*, which recognised the enforceability of emergency arbitrator orders (in the relevant arbitration context), strengthening interim relief effectiveness.

Business meaning: You can get urgent protection faster than a full trial.

Enforcement timelines: what to expect

Let's be straight:

- Arbitration is usually faster than litigation, but it still depends on party cooperation, tribunal discipline, and complexity.
- Challenges and stay tactics exist, but courts have been moving towards requiring serious grounds and structured conditions.

A realistic planning view:

- Simple contractual disputes: months to around 18 months in arbitration (often).
- Complex construction/tech disputes: longer.
- Enforcement/challenge phase: can add time, but courts increasingly limit merits re-litigation under Section 34.

What Indian Courts Will Enforce Strongly

Stronger enforceability

- Clear payment obligations, milestones, interest clauses
- Documented delivery/acceptance mechanisms
- Well-defined termination events and consequences
- Arbitration clauses with clean seat/rules/institution wording
- Security instruments (BG/LC/escrow) that can be triggered cleanly

Weaker / higher-risk enforcement zones

- Vague "best efforts" obligations with no measurable outcomes
- Post-termination non-compete restrictions (often difficult in India)
- Penalty clauses that look punitive rather than compensatory
- Contracts with poor evidence trails (emails/POs not aligned)

Drafting Choices That Make Enforcement Easier in India

If you want contracts to be enforced with minimum drama, your contracts should include:

1. **A clean arbitration clause**
    - institution (ICC/SIAC/LCIA etc.)
    - seat
    - number of arbitrators
    - language
    - interim relief pathway
2. **A payment discipline design**
    - milestones
    - acceptance criteria
    - interest and late-fee structure that is defensible
    - right to suspend supplies/services for non-payment
3. **Security**
    - bank guarantee / LC / escrow triggers
    - step-in rights for key operational contracts
4. **Evidence architecture**
    - document hierarchy clause
    - clear change order mechanism
    - signed acceptance and delivery protocols
5. **A dispute escalation ladder**
    - senior management meeting
    - time-bound negotiation window
    - then arbitration

The "positive side" of India's enforcement reality

Here is the encouraging truth for EU businesses:

1. India's Supreme Court has repeatedly moved arbitration law toward finality and enforceability, especially for foreign awards.
2. Courts have reinforced that Section 34 is not a merits appeal, which protects awards from being re-tried in court.
3. Courts have clarified that they generally cannot "modify" awards like an appellate body—again supporting finality.
4. Interim relief mechanisms have become more practical, including recognition of emergency arbitrator relief in the relevant framework.

How to Build Enforceability Into Transactions From the Start

Contract enforceability in India is not mainly a question of whether courts will uphold a valid agreement—Indian courts do. The real question is whether the contract has been structured to be enforceable in the way the parties will actually need it to be enforced. The contracts that work in India are usually the ones drafted with precision on dispute mechanism, governing law, payment milestones, breach, and remedies.

Forum choice is one of the most important decisions in any India-linked contract. EU companies that default to home-country courts often discover that a European judgement may still require fresh enforcement proceedings in India. Arbitration is usually the more effective route for commercial contracts of significance, particularly where the seat is in a recognised jurisdiction and the award is enforceable in India under the New York Convention framework.

Transaction planning must, therefore, build dispute management into the contract from the beginning. Payment obligations, acceptance criteria, delivery milestones, price adjustment mechanisms, termination consequences, and interim relief strategy should all be drafted clearly. The clearer the contract is on what happens when things go wrong, the easier and less expensive enforcement becomes.

"Enforcement Readiness" Checklist

Before signing:

☐ Arbitration clause: institution + seat + rules + language clearly stated

☐ Interim relief route clearly preserved

☐ Payment milestones + acceptance criteria defined

☐ Interest / late charges drafted conservatively

☐ Evidence trail requirements (PO, delivery, acceptance, change orders)

During performance:

☐ Keep signed acceptance records

☐ Keep change orders documented

☐ Keep emails aligned with contract terms

☐ Maintain a dispute folder from day one

When dispute starts:

☐ Send a clean notice (facts + breach + cure period)

☐ Secure interim relief early if asset risk exists

☐ Avoid emotional correspondence—stick to provable facts

Practical conclusion: If you set up arbitration properly, India is not a "contract enforcement black hole." It is a procedural system that enforces rights when you play it correctly.

Chapter 14

How Do We Retain Control and Protect Our Investment?

Board rights, reserved matters, veto provisions, deadlock mechanisms and exit design.

Control is the most commercially consequential legal concept in cross-border investment, and the most consistently misunderstood. In European legal systems, equity percentage is usually a reliable proxy for decision-making authority. In India, it is not. Control is created by documents, not by percentages. The shareholder agreement, the articles of association, and the board structure determine who actually runs the business and who can block decisions that matter. This chapter explains how to design those documents so that control reflects intent.

One of the biggest misconceptions EU companies carry into India is this:

"If we own the majority, we control the business."

In India, that assumption is often wrong.

Control is not created by shareholding alone. It is created by governance design—how boards are structured, which decisions require consent, how money moves, how information flows, and what happens when parties disagree. Many foreign investors lose practical control in India, not because the law is hostile, but because governance was drafted casually at entry.

This chapter explains how EU companies can retain decision-making power, protect capital, and avoid paralysis, whether they hold a majority stake, a minority stake, or operate through a joint venture.

The Core Reality: Control Is Drafted, Not Assumed

Indian company law allows wide contractual freedom. Shareholders are free to agree on:

1. board composition
2. voting thresholds
3. veto rights
4. information access
5. exit mechanics

Courts and tribunals generally respect these arrangements if they are clearly documented.

Where investors fail is not at law, but at design.

Board Control: Where Real Power Resides

In India, the board is not symbolic. It controls:

1. strategy
2. budgets
3. hiring and firing of key management
4. funding decisions
5. major contracts

If you lose board control, you lose the company, regardless of your shareholding.

Board Composition

EU investors should focus on:

- parity or majority board representation
- nomination rights tied to shareholding
- quorum requirements that require investor presence

A common mistake is allowing the Indian promoter to control:

- board agenda
- meeting schedules
- information circulation

This quietly shifts power.

Practical rule: If a board meeting can happen without you, control is already diluted.

Veto / Reserved Matters: The Real Control Layer

Reserved matters are decisions that cannot be taken without your affirmative vote, regardless of shareholding.

These are the most powerful protection tools for EU investors.

What Must Always Be Reserved

At a minimum, reserved matters should cover:

1. annual budgets and business plans
2. capital expenditure beyond threshold
3. borrowing and security creation
4. related-party transactions
5. changes to share capital
6. appointment/removal of key executives
7. entry into new lines of business
8. major contracts and acquisitions

Without reserved matters, board seats alone are weak.

Majority vs Minority: Control Looks Different

Majority Investor (51%+)

Your risk is not loss of control, it is operational sabotage or delay.

You must protect against:

- management non-cooperation
- information bottlenecks
- local resistance to HQ decisions

Tools that matter:

- clear CEO/CFO appointment rights
- reporting obligations
- escalation mechanisms
- step-in rights

Minority Investor (10%–49%)

Your risk is not daily operations, it is capital misuse and exit blockage.

You must protect against:

- dilution
- asset stripping
- excessive remuneration
- related-party leakage

Minority protection is not about running the company.

It is about preventing value destruction.

Minority Protection: What Indian Law Allows and Enforces

Indian law recognises minority protection strongly, but only if you contract for it.

Key protections include:

1. anti-dilution rights
2. pre-emptive rights on new shares
3. veto on major structural changes
4. information and inspection rights

5. exit rights
6. courts generally enforce these if they are:
7. clear
8. not oppressive
9. not contrary to statute

Information Rights: Control Without Visibility Is Illusion

Many investors focus on voting rights and ignore information rights.

This is a serious mistake.

Without regular, structured information, you cannot:

- detect leakage
- question management decisions
- plan exits
- defend disputes

Information rights should include:

1. monthly management accounts
2. audited annual financials
3. bank statements access
4. related-party transaction details
5. compliance reports

If information is discretionary, control is theoretical.

Deadlocks: The Most Common JV Failure Point

Deadlocks are not rare in India. They are inevitable when:

- parties have equal board power
- reserved matters are extensive
- commercial priorities diverge

What matters is **how the deadlock is resolved**.

Bad Deadlock Design

- endless negotiation
- escalation without consequence
- court litigation

This destroys value.

Good Deadlock Design

- Structured escalation
- time-bound resolution
- economic consequence

Deadlock Resolution Mechanisms That Work

Well-drafted agreements usually include one or more of the following:

1. Escalation to senior leadership
2. Cooling-off period
3. Buy-sell mechanisms (shotgun, Russian roulette)
4. Put / call options
5. Third-party valuation triggers

Deadlocks should **force a result**, not delay it.

Exit Rights: Control at the End Matters Too

Investors often focus on entry control and forget exit control.

Exit rights must be:

- clear
- time-bound
- executable

Common exit tools include:

- IPO rights
- strategic sale rights
- put options
- tag-along and drag-along rights

Without exit clarity, control becomes hostage to cooperation.

Funding Control: How Money Becomes Leverage

Capital infusions are a control lever.

EU investors should ensure:

- funding obligations are proportional
- failure to fund has consequences
- valuation mechanics are pre-agreed

Otherwise, funding rounds become power struggles.

Common Control Mistakes EU Companies Make in India

- assuming shareholding equals control
- accepting "standard" Indian JV templates
- underestimating promoter influence
- weak deadlock clauses
- no exit pressure

These mistakes surface **years later**, when correction is expensive.

What Indian Courts and Tribunals Respect

Indian enforcement forums generally respect:

- board structures agreed by parties
- reserved matters
- veto rights

- exit clauses
- deadlock mechanisms

They do not rescue investors from:

- vague drafting
- incomplete governance design
- optimism-based structures

A Practical Control Framework

Before finalising any India investment, ask:

- Can the board meet without us?
- Can money be spent without our consent?
- Can shares be issued without us?
- Can information be delayed or filtered?
- Can we exit if things stall?

If the answer to any is "yes," control is at risk.

Retaining control in India is not about distrust. It is about designing for reality. Indian businesses are relationship-driven, fast-moving, and entrepreneurial. That energy is an advantage, if governance channels it correctly.

EU companies that succeed in India do not over-lawyer control. They structure it intelligently: strong boards, clear vetoes, real information rights, and decisive deadlock exits. They protect their investment without paralysing the business.

In India, control is not asserted loudly.

It is embedded quietly, on paper, from day one.

SECTION VI

WHAT ABOUT PEOPLE, DATA AND IP?

This section moves from entry strategy to operational exposure across three critical domains—employment, intellectual property, and data governance. Once an EU business begins hiring teams, deploying expatriates, building brand presence, and handling data in India, the core legal risk shifts from regulatory approvals to how these functions are structured, documented, and controlled in practice. It examines how India's employment framework hinges on classification and procedure rather than uniformity, how IP protection depends on early registration and disciplined enforcement rather than reputation, and how data compliance operates as a parallel sovereign framework distinct from GDPR. The objective is not only to access India's talent, market, and digital ecosystem, but to manage them with clarity, contractual precision, and regulatory foresight. In India, operational resilience is not created by assumptions or global templates, but by aligning people strategy, IP ownership, and data governance with local legal realities from the outset.

Chapter 15

How Do Employment and Expatriate Rules Work in India?

Hiring, Termination, Secondments, Visa Categories and Tax Residency Risks

For EU companies entering India, employment decisions often appear straightforward at first glance. Talent is available, hiring is quick, and compensation costs seem competitive.

The real employment risk, however, does not arise at the hiring stage. It surfaces later, during termination, restructuring, secondments, expatriate deployment, and tax scrutiny.

Many foreign companies misjudge this because they apply European employment logic to an Indian system that is fundamentally different in structure, enforcement style, and risk triggers.

"In India, employment risk does not begin at hiring. It begins at the exit."

India is not anti-employer, but it is process-driven, documentation-heavy, and selectively protective.

Understanding India's Employment Framework: The First Reality Check

India does not operate under a single employment law regime. Employment rights and employer obligations depend on the nature of work performed, the role designation, compensation level, and state-specific laws. The most common error EU companies make is assuming uniform treatment across employees. In reality, classification determines everything—from termination rights to litigation exposure.

Broadly, Indian employment law distinguishes between employees who are legally protected as "workmen" and those in managerial or supervisory roles. This distinction is not based on title alone, but on actual job functions. If an employee performs operational, technical, or clerical work, they may fall under the protected category, even if their designation sounds senior. For such employees, termination is tightly regulated, procedural, and often litigated. Conversely, senior managers and executives are governed largely by contract, and courts generally respect well-drafted notice and severance provisions.

Hiring in India: Flexible, but Only if Documented Properly

Hiring in India is commercially flexible, especially for managerial and leadership roles. However, flexibility exists only when employment documentation is clear and disciplined. Informal offer letters, generic templates, or EU-style contracts without India-specific adaptations often become the root cause of disputes years later.

Appointment letters should clearly define the role, reporting structure, place of work, notice periods, termination rights, confidentiality obligations, and intellectual property ownership. Courts and tribunals in India rely heavily on what is written. Ambiguity usually benefits the employee, not the employer. For EU companies, investing time in clean employment documentation at entry avoids disproportionate risk at exit.

Termination: Procedural, Not Prohibited

Contrary to common perception, terminating employees in India is not impossible. It is procedural. For senior and managerial employees, termination generally works smoothly when notice requirements are followed, dues are settled promptly, and the process is respectful and documented. Problems arise when terminations are abrupt, poorly communicated, or inconsistent with contract terms.

For employees classified as "workmen," termination is significantly more regulated. Statutory notice, compensation, and, in some cases, government intimation are mandatory. Courts may order reinstatement if the procedure is violated. EU companies must therefore identify early whether any roles fall within this protected category and structure workforce planning accordingly.

> ***"You can terminate employment in India, but never carelessly."***

Secondments: Useful, but Structurally Sensitive

Secondments are commonly used by EU companies during market entry or transition phases. While commercially convenient, secondments are one of the highest-risk employment structures if not designed carefully. Indian authorities assess secondments based on economic reality rather than labels, looking at who controls daily work, who bears cost, and where the employee is functionally integrated.

If the Indian entity effectively controls the secondee, the individual may be treated as an Indian employee for labour, tax and social security purposes, regardless of home payroll arrangements. Poorly structured secondments can also create permanent establishment exposure for the EU parent. Best practice involves clear secondment agreements, limited duration, transparent cost recharge, aligned supervision structures, and compliance with Indian payroll or social security rules where required.

> ***"A secondment is not just a people's decision. It is a tax and control decision."***

Expatriates: Where Immigration, Employment and Tax Intersect

Deploying expatriates into India requires managing three overlapping regimes simultaneously: immigration law, employment law, and taxation. Visa misuse is a common and serious issue. Business visas do not permit employment activities, and working under the wrong visa category can result in fines, deportation, and blacklisting.

From a tax perspective, expatriates create risk based on days spent in India, nature of duties performed, and salary structure. Even short-term presence can trigger personal tax liability and employer withholding obligations. More critically, expatriates who negotiate contracts, manage operations, or represent the EU parent commercially can create permanent establishment risk, exposing the parent entity to Indian corporate tax.

Independent Contractors and Consultants: Not a Safe Shortcut

Using consultants instead of employees is common but risky. Indian authorities look beyond labels to assess control, exclusivity, and integration. Contractors who function like employees may be reclassified, triggering labour and tax liabilities. This risk increases when consultants work exclusively, follow company working hours, or perform core business functions.

Statutory Benefits, IP, and Confidentiality

India mandates certain employee benefits, such as gratuity and leave entitlements. These are statutory obligations, not discretionary perks, and long-term liabilities can accumulate silently. Concerning intellectual property, EU companies must not assume automatic ownership of employee-created IP. Ownership must be expressly addressed in contracts, with confidentiality obligations surviving termination. Courts enforce what is written—not what is assumed.

"In India, assumptions do not protect employers, contracts do."

The Positive Reality for EU Employers

Despite its complexity, India offers significant advantages: a deep talent pool, flexibility in hiring senior professionals, and increasingly predictable outcomes when documentation and procedure are followed. Employment disputes usually arise not from hostile laws, but from poor planning and casual execution. Companies that invest in structured employment frameworks find India scalable and manageable.

Employment and Expatriate Readiness Checklist

Before Hiring

☐ Identify whether the role may fall under the "workman" category.

☐ Issue a detailed appointment letter (role, notice, termination, IP).

☐ Align job description with actual functions.

During Employment

☐ Maintain clear reporting and performance records.

☐ Track statutory benefits and accruals

☐ Ensure compliance with state-specific labour laws.

For Termination

☐ Follow notice and severance strictly as per contract

☐ Document reasons and process

☐ Settle dues promptly and formally

For Secondments / Expatriates

☐ Correct visa category obtained

☐ Secondment agreement executed

☐ Tax residency and day-count tracked

☐ PE risk assessed

☐ Social security obligations reviewed

For Consultants

☐ Independence and non-exclusivity ensured

☐ No employee-like control or integration

Employment law in India is not anti-business. It is procedural, protective in defined areas, and unforgiving of informality. EU companies that understand classification, respect process, and document relationships clearly retain flexibility while avoiding disputes. People strategy in India is not about cost arbitrage; it is about control, compliance, and foresight.

Handled correctly, Indian teams become a growth engine.

Handled casually, they become a long-term liability.

Chapter 16

How Do We Protect Our Brand and Intellectual Property (IP) in India?

First-to-file trademarks, technology transfer safeguards, distributor IP risk.

For EU companies entering India, brand and intellectual property are often the most valuable assets they bring into the market—and also the most exposed. India is a fast-growing, consumption-led economy with strong entrepreneurial energy. That same energy also creates imitation risk. The widespread belief that IP protection in India is weak is only partly true.

The more accurate position is this: India protects IP seriously, but only when owners register early, enforce consistently, and structure relationships carefully.

IP protection in India is less about theory and more about discipline.

> ***"In India, unregistered IP is invisible IP."***

Registration is the Foundation, Not a Formality

India operates a registration-centric IP regime. Unlike some EU jurisdictions, where reputation and prior use carry substantial weight, Indian courts, customs authorities, and enforcement agencies rely heavily on formal registration records. If a trademark, design, or patent is not registered in India, enforcement becomes slower, weaker, and more expensive. EU companies often delay registration until the market proves itself. In India, that delay opens the door to trademark squatters, copycats, and even well-meaning distributors registering IP in their own name "for convenience."

Trademarks: The First and Most Critical Defence

Trademarks are the most frequently infringed IP right in India, and also the easiest to protect if registered early. India follows a first-to-file system, meaning priority is based on filing, not reputation abroad. Registration is class-specific and should cover word marks, logos, slogans, packaging elements, and in some cases, trade dress. While Indian law recognises "well-known marks," obtaining that status takes time and evidence. For new entrants, early filing remains the safest strategy.

"If you do not register your trademark in India, someone else may."

Patents, Designs and Copyright: Visibility Matters

Patent and design protection in India are effective, but timing is critical. Public disclosure before filing can destroy patent or design rights. EU companies often focus on patents while ignoring design registrations, even though counterfeiting in India frequently copies visual appearance rather than technical function. Copyright protection arises automatically, but registration and clear ownership records significantly improve enforcement. This is particularly relevant for software, manuals, training materials, and marketing content. Ownership must be clearly assigned in employment and contractor agreements; assumptions based on EU practice do not hold automatically.

Partners and Distributors: The Most Overlooked IP Risk

One of the most serious IP risks in India does not come from unknown counterfeiters, but from commercial partners. Distributors and licensees often have deep market access and visibility. Without strict contractual boundaries, this access can turn into misuse—such as registering trademarks locally, exceeding licence scope, or continuing brand use after termination. EU companies must ensure that IP ownership is clearly retained, usage is licensed and limited, and termination consequences are explicit and enforceable.

"Your biggest IP risk in India is often your own business partner."

Counterfeiting and Enforcement: Practical, Not Perfect

Counterfeiting exists in India, but enforcement is more effective than commonly perceived when approached correctly. Civil courts are generally willing to grant interim injunctions, including search and seizure orders, when IP is registered and evidence is clear. Criminal remedies are available in serious cases, and enforcement agencies do act when complaints are well-prepared. The key variables are speed, documentation, and consistency. Delay or informal tolerance weakens enforcement credibility.

Customs and Online Enforcement: Underused but Powerful Tools

Customs recordation of registered trademarks is one of the most underused IP tools in India. Once recorded, customs authorities can detain suspected infringing imports at the border, often stopping counterfeits before they reach the market. Similarly, Indian courts have become increasingly proactive in online enforcement. They issue takedown orders, block infringing listings, and direct e-commerce platforms to disclose seller details, provided the IP owner acts promptly and presents clear registration and infringement evidence.

"Customs enforcement often stops counterfeits before courts ever see them."

Internal IP Leakage: Employees and Contractors

> ***"In India, IP ownership must be written, not assumed."***

Another underestimated risk is internal IP leakage. Employee-created IP does not automatically vest in the employer unless contracts clearly state so. Confidentiality, non-misuse, and post-termination obligations must be drafted precisely and enforced consistently. Access to sensitive data should be controlled operationally, not just contractually. Without these safeguards, enforcement becomes reactive and uncertain.

What the Enforcement Reality Actually Looks Like

Indian courts and authorities generally act decisively when four conditions are met: the IP is registered, ownership is clear, infringement evidence is documented, and enforcement action is timely. They are far less sympathetic when registration is missing, delay suggests acquiescence, or contracts are vague. The system rewards preparation and consistency rather than brand size or foreign origin.

A Practical IP Strategy for EU Companies

A workable IP strategy in India rests on four pillars: early registration, strong contractual controls, continuous market monitoring, and swift enforcement. IP protection is not a one-time legal exercise; it is an ongoing business process that must scale with operations.

India IP Protection Checklist

Before Market Entry

☐ Register trademarks (word marks, logos, packaging) in relevant classes

☐ File patents and designs before public disclosure

☐ Document copyright ownership for software and content

Contractual Safeguards

☐ Clear IP ownership clauses

☐ Limited licence language for distributors and partners

☐ Post-termination brand and IP restrictions

☐ Confidentiality obligations with survival

Operational Controls

☐ Restrict access to sensitive IP

☐ Train employees and partners on brand usage

☐ Monitor offline and online marketplaces

Enforcement Readiness

☐ Customs IP recordation completed

☐ Evidence collection process defined

☐ Enforcement counsel identified

India does not require aggressive IP protection strategies. It requires early action, disciplined registration, and structured relationships. The companies that face the greatest losses are not those whose IP is infringed, but those who delay protection until infringement becomes visible.

In India, brand value grows fast.

So does imitation.

Chapter 17

How Do Data Protection and Digital Laws Affect Us?

DPDPA vs GDPR, data localisation, cross-border transfers and sector-specific rules.

For many EU companies, data risk in India is underestimated. The assumption is simple: *"We already comply with GDPR, so India should be manageable."* This assumption is only partially correct. While India's data framework borrows concepts from GDPR, its enforcement logic, government access powers, sectoral rules, and compliance triggers are different.

India does not treat data protection as a purely privacy issue. It treats data as a sovereign, economic and security asset. This difference matters deeply for IT, SaaS, fintech, healthcare, telecom, manufacturing platforms, and any business that processes customer, employee, or operational data.

This chapter explains how India's Data Law: Digital Personal Data Protection Act 2023 (DPDPA), works in practice, where they overlap with GDPR, where they diverge, and what foreign companies must put in place before entering India.

The Core Reality: GDPR Compliance Is Helpful, but Not Sufficient

GDPR gives EU companies a strong compliance foundation. However:

- India's law focuses more on state interests and enforcement powers
- Sector regulators in India often impose stricter operational rules
- Data localisation expectations exist in specific sectors

- Penalties are not only financial, they can also include operational disruption

India does not require perfection. It requires traceability, control, and accountability.

India's Data Protection Landscape

India's data protection and digital compliance framework operates across three overlapping layers: general personal data protection law, sector-specific regulatory requirements, and IT / cybersecurity obligations.

Businesses entering India must assess all three together, because compliance under one layer does not remove exposure under the others.

Companies are often compliant with one layer and exposed in another.

GDPR vs India Data Protection Framework

Aspect	GDPR (EU)	India Data Protection Framework
Philosophy	Individual privacy rights	Privacy + sovereignty + security
Scope	Personal data of EU individuals	Digital personal data processed in India
Consent	Detailed, granular	Consent-based but more flexible
Data localisation	Generally not mandatory	Mandatory / expected in some sectors
Cross-border transfer	Permitted with safeguards	Permitted, but sector restrictions apply
Regulator approach	Independent data authorities	Government-appointed authority
Enforcement style	Rights-driven	Compliance + security-driven
Breach reporting	Strict timelines	Mandatory with government visibility
Government access	Limited, regulated	Wider statutory access powers

Key takeaway:

GDPR compliance helps, but India requires additional controls and local readiness.

Critical Provisions of India's Data Privacy Laws and Consequences

Provision Area	What India Requires	Consequence of Non-Compliance
Lawful processing	Clear purpose + consent	Penalties, orders to stop processing
Data minimisation	Collect only what is necessary	Regulatory scrutiny
Breach reporting	Mandatory reporting to authority	Fines + operational investigation
Data security	Reasonable security safeguards	Liability + audits
Government access	Compliance with lawful requests	Criminal and civil exposure
Children's data	Higher protection standards	Heavy penalties
Processor obligations	Contractual safeguards	Joint liability
Cross-border transfers	Allowed but monitored	Transfer restrictions
Consent withdrawal	Must be honoured	Orders to delete / restrict data

Sector-Specific Data Risks

1. IT, SaaS, and Platforms

For IT, SaaS and platform businesses, data risk in India often arises quietly. Data may be hosted outside India but accessed by Indian users or handled by India-based support teams. Logs, metadata and telemetry – often treated as technical data – can still qualify as personal data. Without clear mapping of data flows and team roles, companies face overlapping exposure across privacy compliance, tax permanent establishment and regulatory scrutiny.

2. Fintech, Payments, and BFSI

Fintech, payments, and BFSI businesses face some of the strictest data expectations in India. Regulators place strong emphasis on data localisation, audit readiness, and vendor oversight. Breach reporting timelines are tight, and cloud arrangements are closely examined. Companies that enter India without architecture aligned to regulatory expectations often find themselves forced to redesign systems post-entry, which is costly, disruptive, and difficult to execute without affecting customers.

3. Healthcare and Life Sciences

In healthcare and life sciences, data risk is amplified because personal and health data are treated as highly sensitive. Consent standards are stricter, storage and access controls are closely monitored, and regulators take a proactive stance. Any breach, misuse, or ambiguity in data handling can trigger investigations or directions to suspend processing. For these sectors, data compliance failures do not just attract penalties; they can directly interrupt core business operations.

4. Manufacturing, IoT, and Smart Systems

Manufacturing and IoT-driven businesses often underestimate data exposure because their focus is on machines rather than individuals. In practice, machine data frequently overlaps with employee data, access logs, and operational analytics. Cybersecurity incident reporting obligations apply, and poorly protected systems increase IP leakage risk. Data compliance gaps usually arise not from customer data, but from operational data flows that were never treated as regulated information.

Cloud, Hosting, and Tech Stack Risks

India does not prohibit the use of foreign cloud providers, but it does expect cloud choices to align with sector policy and regulatory needs. Certain regulators require India-based storage, and incident reporting obligations apply regardless of where data is hosted. Contracts must permit lawful access and disclosures to authorities. Cloud decisions, driven purely by cost or global standardisation, often require painful corrections once regulatory scrutiny begins.

The Real Enforcement Risk in India

Indian authorities rarely begin enforcement with heavy penalties. They usually start with information requests, audits, and compliance directions. However, if these are delayed, ignored, or handled casually, enforcement escalates quickly into fines, restrictions on data processing, or operational limitations. In India, the biggest risk is not the monetary penalty; it is business disruption caused by regulatory intervention at critical moments.

India Data Protection and Digital Law Readiness Checklist

Governance

☐ Data mapping completed (what, where, who, why)

☐ Data protection officer / responsible function identified

☐ Incident response plan defined

Legal and Contractual

☐ India-specific privacy notices drafted

☐ Processor and cloud contracts updated

☐ Lawful access and disclosure clauses included

Technology

☐ Data security controls documented

☐ Access controls and logging in place

☐ Backup and recovery tested

Cross-Border

☐ Transfer mechanisms assessed

☐ Sector localisation rules checked

☐ EU–India data flow alignment confirmed

Sector Readiness

Fintech / health / telecom rules mapped (if applicable)

☐ Regulator engagement strategy defined

What EU Companies Should Do Before Entry

Before entering India, companies should:

- complete a data flow and localisation impact assessment
- adjust contracts—not just policies
- align cloud architecture with sector rules
- train India teams on incident reporting obligations

Data risk in India is not theoretical, it is operational.

Closing Perspective

India does not reject global digital business. It expects it to operate with accountability, traceability, and respect for national regulatory priorities. GDPR gives EU companies a strong starting point, but not a complete solution.

Those who treat India's data laws as an extension of GDPR, struggle later.

Those who treat them as a parallel, sovereign framework, operate smoothly.

In India, data compliance is not a legal exercise.

It is a business continuity decision.

SECTION VII

HOW DOES THIS PLAY OUT BY SECTOR?

This section moves from market opportunity to sector-specific execution risk, where the real exposure for EU companies in India lies not in entry, but in how operations are structured and managed. It highlights how manufacturing depends on land diligence, approvals, and localisation planning; healthcare on pricing controls, regulatory expansion, and liability; auto and engineering on supplier strength, tariffs, and phased localisation; and IT/SaaS on permanent establishment, tax characterisation, and contract clarity. The objective is not just to operate in India, but to do so with integrated control across regulatory, commercial, and operational layers. In India, sector success is driven less by strategy and more by disciplined execution across every moving part.

Chapter 18

What Should Manufacturing and Industrial Companies Know Before Setting Up in India?

Land, factories, environment, localisation, China-plus-one strategy, and stability argument.

For EU manufacturing and industrial companies, India represents scale, cost efficiency, and long-term market depth. But manufacturing entry into India is not just a commercial decision—it is a land, infrastructure, regulatory, and execution project. Many foreign manufacturers underestimate this because they compare India to EU industrial zones where approvals are centralised, timelines are predictable, and utilities are plug-and-play. India works differently.

This chapter explains what manufacturing companies must understand before committing capital: how land is acquired, how factories are approved, how environmental and local compliance shapes timelines, and why localisation decisions determine success or frustration.

> ***"In India, manufacturing success is decided before the first machine is installed."***

Land: The First and Most Critical Decision

Land selection in India is not merely about price per square metre. It determines approvals, timelines, tax incentives, labour access, and even litigation risk. EU companies often assume industrial land is "clean" if it is within an industrial zone. That assumption can be dangerous.

Key land-related realities include:

- Land titles must be verified thoroughly
- Land-use classification must permit the intended activity
- Local zoning and development plans matter
- State-level incentives vary significantly

Acquiring land without title diligence or zoning clarity is one of the costliest mistakes foreign manufacturers make in India.

Factories and Construction: Approval-Heavy but Predictable if Planned

Constructing a factory in India requires multiple approvals, often obtained in parallel rather than sequentially. These typically include:

- factory licence
- building plan approvals
- fire safety clearances
- power and water connections,

Delays usually occur not because approvals are denied, but because documentation is inconsistent or assumptions are made about "standard" timelines. Local engagement and sequencing matter more than speed.

Environmental Compliance: Non-Negotiable and Increasingly Strict

Environmental regulation is one of the most underestimated risk areas for industrial companies. India classifies industries into categories based on pollution potential, and approvals depend on:

- type of manufacturing
- capacity

- emissions and waste
- location sensitivity

Environmental clearance is not a formality. It affects plant design, equipment choice and operating costs.

"Environmental compliance in India is not a checkbox, it is a design input."

Localisation: More Than Just Sourcing

Localisation is often discussed as a cost or incentive topic. In practice, it impacts:

- customs duty exposure
- FTA-benefit eligibility
- supply-chain resilience
- government perception

Many EU manufacturers enter India as import-heavy operations and later struggle to localise under pressure. Those who plan localisation early, gradually shifting sourcing, assembly, or value addition, face fewer disruptions and gain pricing flexibility.

Labour and Industrial Relations: Practical, Not Ideological

India has a large manufacturing workforce, but labour availability varies by region and skill set. Industrial relations are generally stable when:

- wages are competitive
- statutory benefits are respected
- local workforce expectations are understood

Problems usually arise when companies apply EU shop-floor practices without adapting to Indian labour law structure and cultural expectations.

Utilities and Infrastructure: Plan Buffers

Power, water and logistics infrastructure differ widely across states and industrial parks. While many industrial zones are well developed, redundancy planning is essential. Backup power, water sourcing and logistics alternatives should be built into the project cost from the start.

Case Study 1: German Engineering Company (Planned Success)

A German industrial equipment manufacturer chose land within a state-promoted industrial corridor and completed title checks, zoning verification, and environmental scoping before acquisition. The factory was designed in line with environmental norms from the outset. As a result, approvals were received within planned timelines, no post-construction changes were required, and commissioning proceeded smoothly. Early diligence and design alignment significantly reduced execution risk.

Case Study 2: Italian Manufacturing Unit (Delayed Entry)

An Italian mid-sized manufacturer acquired land through a local intermediary, assuming approvals would follow automatically. Post-acquisition zoning restrictions required a formal change of land use approval, which took over a year. During this period, capital remained locked, construction costs escalated, and market entry was delayed. The case highlights that land appearing industrial may not always be legally suitable for manufacturing activities.

Case Study 3: French Chemical Processing Company (Compliance-Driven Redesign)

A French chemical company underestimated India's environmental approval requirements and submitted plant designs that did not meet emission norms. Regulators required a redesign after submission, leading to additional capital expenditure, approval delays, and increased regulatory scrutiny. The experience underscores that in India, environmental clearance is not procedural—it directly shapes plant design and must be integrated from the planning stage.

> ***"In India, regulatory delay is usually the cost of late planning."***

The Positive Reality for Industrial Companies

India actively wants manufacturing investment. Many states offer:

- capital subsidies
- tax incentives
- infrastructure support
- single-window facilitation

Companies that engage early with state authorities and align projects with policy objectives, often receive strong institutional support.

What Usually Goes Wrong

Manufacturing projects fail or stall when:

- land diligence is skipped
- approvals are treated sequentially instead of parallel
- environmental compliance is underestimated
- localisation is delayed too long
- timelines are driven by optimism, not regulation

These are avoidable issues.

India is not a difficult manufacturing destination. It is a detail-sensitive one. EU industrial companies that plan land, approvals, environment, and localisation together, not in silos, execute faster and scale more confidently.

Manufacturing in India rewards preparation, not shortcuts.

Those who respect the process, build durable operations.

Those who rush it pay for time later.

India as a China-Plus-One Manufacturing Base

For many EU manufacturers, India is no longer just a domestic market. It is a production alternative. As supply-chain concentration risk in China has become a board-level issue, India has moved from a secondary option to an active manufacturing consideration across electronics, chemicals, pharmaceuticals, automotive components, and industrial equipment.

Why India is being evaluated seriously:

- large and scalable workforce
- lower labour cost than many competing markets
- technical and managerial talent available in English
- Production Linked Incentive (PLI) schemes in priority sectors
- improving trade economics under the India–EU FTA

"India is not replacing every China-linked supply chain, but for many EU companies, it is becoming the most credible second manufacturing base."

For EU companies, the practical attraction is not only cost; it is diversification. A manufacturing base in India can reduce overdependence on one geography, improve supply-chain resilience, and create optionality for serving both India and export markets.

India as a Stability-Linked Production Option in an Uncertain World

India's manufacturing case is not only about cost and scale. It is also about stability. In a world shaped by sanctions risk, export controls, shipping disruption, and geopolitical tension, EU manufacturers are looking for production locations that offer both commercial depth and strategic reliability.

India's practical strengths include:

- democratic and rules-based institutional framework.
- no comparable sanctions exposure to several other large markets.
- functioning contract, IP and arbitration systems.

- policy support for long-term manufacturing investment.
- growing strategic alignment with Europe through the FTA.

This does not mean India is frictionless. It means the risks are more manageable when the investment is structured properly. For long-term manufacturing businesses, that matters.

"India is not only a cost-efficient production option, it is increasingly a stability-linked manufacturing choice in an uncertain global market."

Sector-Specific Approval Checklists

A. Heavy Manufacturing / Engineering / Automotive

☐ Industrial land title and zoning clearance

☐ Factory licence under local factories law

☐ Building plan approval

☐ Fire safety clearance

☐ Power and water connection approvals

☐ Labour law registrations

☐ State incentive registration

B. Process Industries / Chemicals / Pharma Manufacturing

☐ Environmental clearance (as per category)

☐ Consent to Establish and Consent to Operate

☐ Hazardous waste authorisation

☐ Pollution control board approvals

☐ Factory licence

☐ Fire and safety approvals

☐ Storage and transport permits

C. Electronics / Industrial Technology / Assembly Units

☐ Industrial land or SEZ approval

☐ Factory registration

☐ Electrical safety approvals

☐ Import-export code

☐ Customs bonding (if applicable)

☐ Labour registrations

☐ Incentive scheme approvals

Why This Matters for EU Manufacturers

Taken together, these factors change how India should be viewed. It is not only a place to sell into, but also a place to build from. EU manufacturers that treat India as part of a long-term production strategy—not just a market-entry strategy—are likely to gain more value from both localisation and the FTA.

Chapter 19

What Are the Key Risks for Pharma and Medical Devices?

NPPA pricing controls, CDSCO registration, liability allocation and tariff interaction.

India is one of the largest and fastest-growing healthcare markets globally. For EU pharmaceutical and medical device companies, it offers scale, clinical demand, manufacturing depth, and long-term growth. At the same time, India applies a public-interest-first regulatory philosophy, where affordability, access, and patient safety often override pure commercial considerations.

This does not mean India is hostile to foreign healthcare companies. It means the rules of the game are different. Companies that plan for these differences build durable businesses. Those that assume European regulatory comfort will carry over often face disruption.

> ***"In India, healthcare regulation is driven by public interest first, commercial interest second."***

This chapter focuses on three non-negotiable risk areas that define outcomes in India's healthcare sector: pricing controls, regulatory expansion, and liability exposure, illustrated with real market cases.

1. Pricing Controls: The Biggest Commercial Shock for Foreign Pharma

India regulates prices of medicines and certain medical devices through statutory mechanisms that allow authorities to fix ceiling prices, cap trade margins, and even mandate retrospective price adjustments. Unlike EU systems that rely on negotiated reimbursement and market segmentation, India follows a direct intervention model driven by affordability and public interest. Pricing controls can be imposed after a product has already achieved commercial success, which means that pricing freedom in India is conditional rather than permanent and must be factored into long-term commercial planning.

Real Market Case: Roche's Herceptin and Oncology Pricing

Roche's anti-cancer drug Herceptin became a high-profile example of India's approach to pricing intervention in life-saving therapies. High prices triggered public interest litigation, policy debate, and discussions around compulsory licensing. Although compulsory licensing was not ultimately imposed, sustained regulatory scrutiny and public pressure led to alternative access and pricing models. The case established a clear precedent: in India, commercial success in critical and high-impact therapies often attracts regulatory intervention aimed at balancing innovation with affordability.

"If a drug becomes essential in India, price freedom becomes conditional."

2. Medical Devices Pricing: A Hard Lesson from Orthopaedics

India's approach to medical device pricing became clear when the government imposed statutory ceiling prices on coronary stents and later on orthopaedic knee implants. These interventions were driven by affordability and patient access concerns and applied across the market, including multinational manufacturers. Unlike markets where advanced devices are priced primarily on innovation and brand positioning, India showed that once a device is treated as an essential healthcare product with widespread clinical use, it may be brought under direct price control measures.

Real Market Case: Cardiac Stents and Knee Implants

The price caps on coronary stents and knee implants materially altered pricing freedom for multinational device companies, reduced margins, and limited distributor and hospital-level mark-ups. The larger lesson for EU medical device businesses is clear: in India, commercial success in a clinically important product category does not prevent later price intervention. It can increase that risk.

> ***"In India, medical devices are regulated like medicines once scale is achieved."***

3. Regulation: When the Rules Change After Entry

The Reality

India's regulatory framework for medical devices has expanded steadily over the last decade as the sector moved from light oversight to structured regulation. Product categories that were once outside formal control have been progressively brought under approval, licensing, and post-market surveillance requirements. This evolution reflects India's policy shift towards stronger patient safety and quality standards. For foreign manufacturers, this means that regulatory compliance in India is not static; it evolves with market maturity and public health priorities.

Real Market Case: Sudden Device Re-classification

Several imported medical devices entered India during a period of minimal regulation. When new medical device rules were later notified, entire product categories were suddenly required to obtain fresh approvals, undergo quality audits, and submit detailed compliance documentation. Companies that had not anticipated this regulatory expansion faced temporary sales suspensions and supply-chain disruptions. The episode underlines a critical lesson for market entrants: India's regulatory perimeter expands over time, and entry strategies must be built for future regulation, not current regulatory comfort.

> ***"In India, regulatory compliance is not static, it expands."***

4. Liability Exposure: When Brand Owners Are Pulled In

The Reality

India's healthcare liability environment has moved towards stronger patient protection and accountability. While India does not operate through US-style mass tort litigation, courts, regulators, and government authorities increasingly focus on patient safety, informed consent, product warnings, and post-market conduct. In serious product-failure cases, exposure is no longer confined to direct contractual relationships. Brand owners and manufacturers may face scrutiny for design, warnings, monitoring, and corrective response, particularly where devices are widely used or linked to significant adverse outcomes.

Real Market Case: ASR Hip Implant Litigation

The ASR hip implant matter involving Johnson & Johnson / DePuy in India shows how liability and compensation exposure can attach at the manufacturer and brand level. The episode led to recalls, a government-backed compensation framework, years of proceedings, and reputational harm. Although hospitals and surgeons formed part of the treatment chain, Indian regulatory and compensation processes placed substantial accountability on the manufacturer/importer side.

"In healthcare disputes, Indian authorities look beyond contracts to patient impact."

The lesson for foreign healthcare companies is clear: in India, liability risk does not stop with the distributor or medical intermediary; it can travel back to the brand.

5. Advertising, Promotion, and Claims: Silent Exposure

India applies strict controls on pharmaceutical and medical device advertising, particularly around therapeutic claims, off-label promotion, and comparative advertising. Practices that may be acceptable in other jurisdictions, such as aggressive scientific detailing or implied superiority claims, can attract regulatory action and public scrutiny in India.

Enforcement is often triggered not by competitors, but by regulators, consumer groups, or public interest litigation. For foreign companies, this creates a silent but serious exposure. The key lesson is clear: in India, marketing compliance is as critical as product approval itself.

6. Distribution and Hospital Interface Risk

EU pharmaceutical and medical device companies often rely extensively on local distributors and hospital procurement teams to access the Indian market. This reliance creates risk when distributors over-promise capabilities, pricing, or outcomes, or when hospitals expect support that goes beyond contractual commitments. Inadequate training, documentation, or oversight can quickly translate into compliance breaches or liability exposure. Indian authorities and courts frequently look beyond contractual allocations to assess actual conduct. Strong contractual controls, clear role definitions, and regular compliance training are essential to manage this interface effectively.

The Positive Reality for EU Healthcare Companies

Despite these risks, India offers:

- predictable enforcement once rules are understood
- growing respect for registered IP
- increasing regulatory transparency
- long-term demand stability

Companies that align pricing strategy with public interest, treat regulation as continuous and manage liability proactively succeed over decades.

How Tariffs, Registration, Liability and Pricing Controls Interact in Practice

For EU pharmaceutical and medical device companies, tariff reduction under the India–EU FTA is commercially relevant, but it does not operate in isolation. In India, pricing, registration, liability, and post-market compliance affect whether tariff savings actually convert into business value.

Tariff savings do not always create pricing freedom.

In pharmaceuticals, the NLEM and NPPA framework can restrict how far lower landed cost can be translated into market pricing. In many cases, tariff reduction improves margin rather than competitive pricing flexibility. That remains commercially useful, but only if the India pricing model has been built around regulatory controls from the start.

Registration controls commercial timing.

FTA access does not override CDSCO approval. A product approved in Europe cannot be sold in India until Indian registration, labelling, and regulatory requirements are completed. For many drugs and devices, that process can materially delay launch. Companies that begin CDSCO engagement late often lose the first real phase of market opportunity.

Liability and pricing risk must be planned together.

India's healthcare sector carries increasing exposure around recalls, adverse event reporting, post-market surveillance, and product liability. At the same time, pricing controls can expand to additional products. EU companies, therefore, need more than a tariff strategy. They need a coordinated India strategy covering registration timing, pricing scenarios, liability allocation, insurance coverage, and distribution controls.

"In India, healthcare success is not about speed. It is about credibility, compliance and continuity."

The practical lesson is clear:

Tariff improvement helps, but in India, it delivers value only when registration, liability, and pricing control risk are built into the same market-entry model.

Pharma and Medical Devices Risk-Readiness Checklist

Pricing and Commercial

☐ Pricing model stress-tested for price control

☐ Distributor margins aligned with capped scenarios

☐ No long-term fixed pricing without adjustment rights

Regulatory

☐ Product classification reviewed annually

☐ Post-market surveillance systems active

☐ India-specific marketing compliance review

Liability and Risk

☐ India-specific product liability insurance

☐ Adverse event reporting protocol

☐ Training obligations documented and audited

Governance

☐ Central oversight on regulatory filings

☐ Board visibility on pricing and liability risks

☐ Crisis response plan defined

India is not a hostile healthcare market. It is a serious and principled one. It expects foreign pharma and medical device companies to match commercial ambition with public responsibility.

EU companies that plan for pricing controls, accept regulatory expansion as part of the market, and manage liability proactively, do not merely survive in India—they build trusted, long-term franchises.

Chapter 20

What Challenges Do Auto and Engineering Companies Face?

Tariff planning, localisation roadmap, supplier risk, and logistics resilience.

India is one of the world's most complex automotive and engineering markets. It is large, cost-sensitive, fast-scaling and deeply policy-driven. For EU auto OEMs and engineering companies, India offers long-term demand, manufacturing depth and export potential, but it also brings a set of structural challenges that are often underestimated.

"In India's auto sector, supply chains fail faster than factories."

The biggest mistakes EU companies make in India's auto and engineering sector are not technical. They are supply-chain, policy, and planning mistakes. This chapter focuses on three pressure points that determine success or failure: supplier risk, localisation norms, and tariff planning, and how to manage them realistically.

1. Supplier Risk: The Hidden Operational Exposure

The Reality

India has a deep supplier ecosystem, but it is highly fragmented. Quality, compliance maturity, and financial strength vary widely across Tier-1, Tier-2, and Tier-3 suppliers. EU companies often assume that once a supplier is approved, risk is under control. In India, supplier risk is dynamic, not static.

Common supplier risks include:

- inconsistent quality
- overdependence on single vendors
- weak financial resilience
- poor labour compliance
- inability to scale with volume

When suppliers fail, OEMs and integrators carry the operational and reputational fallout.

Real Market Case: Tier-2 Supplier Failure Impacting OEM Production

Several global auto OEMs operating in India have faced production disruptions due to Tier-2 suppliers defaulting during periods of demand fluctuation. Financial stress at lower tiers led to:

- missed deliveries
- quality failures
- line stoppages

Lesson: Supplier due diligence in India must extend beyond Tier-1.

"In India, your weakest supplier defines your strongest risk."

2. Localisation Norms: Policy-Driven, Not Optional

The Reality

Localisation in India is not just a cost or efficiency decision—it is a policy lever. Government incentives, procurement access, and even market perception increasingly depend on:

- local value addition
- domestic sourcing
- phased manufacturing programmes

EU companies that rely heavily on imports often face:

- higher tariffs
- limited incentive access
- political and regulatory scrutiny

Localisation is expected to increase over time, not remain static.

Real Market Case: Auto OEMs and Phased Manufacturing

Several global OEMs entering India initially relied on imported kits. Over time, policy pressure forced rapid localisation of components. Companies that planned localisation early adapted smoothly. Those that delayed faced:

- margin compression
- renegotiation with suppliers
- operational disruption

Lesson: Localisation should be planned as a roadmap, not a reaction.

"In India, localisation is a journey that policy will push you to complete."

3. Engineering and Auto Tariff Planning: The Margin Battleground

The Reality

Tariffs in India's auto and engineering sector are not neutral. They are designed to:

- discourage finished imports
- promote domestic manufacturing
- reward value addition

EU companies often misprice products by assuming stable tariff regimes. In reality:

- tariffs change
- classifications are scrutinised
- customs audits are frequent

FTA benefits, where applicable, do not eliminate the need for careful tariff engineering.

Real Market Case: Import-Heavy Strategy Becoming Unviable

Multiple global OEMs and component manufacturers have exited or restructured India operations after relying too long on import-heavy models. Rising tariffs and reduced incentives made pricing unsustainable.

"In India, tariffs are not just taxes, they are industrial signals."

Lesson: Tariff planning must align with localisation strategy.

4. Engineering Services and Technology Transfer Risk

EU engineering companies often bring proprietary designs, processes and know-how into India. Risks arise when:

- IP boundaries are unclear
- suppliers reverse-engineer components
- technology transfer is not phased

Contracts must clearly define:

- ownership
- usage limits
- post-termination restrictions

5. Quality, Compliance, and Recall Exposure

Indian consumers and regulators are increasingly intolerant of quality failures. Product recalls in the auto and engineering sector attract:

- regulatory scrutiny
- media attention
- brand damage

Quality control must extend deep into the supplier chain.

"In India, quality failures travel upstream to the brand owner."

The Positive Reality for EU Auto and Engineering Companies

Despite these challenges, India remains one of the most promising auto and engineering markets globally because:

- demand is structural, not cyclical
- supplier capability improves rapidly with engagement
- government actively supports manufacturing
- export integration is growing

Companies that plan supplier strategy, localisation, and tariffs together, not in silos, build resilient operations.

Post-FTA Priorities for Auto and Engineering Companies

The India–EU FTA improves the commercial case for auto components and engineering goods, but it does not simplify the sector. For EU companies, the post-FTA question is not only whether tariffs will be reduced, it is how those tariff changes interact with localisation pressure, supplier capability, and logistics resilience.

Tariff planning becomes more important, not less.

Companies must map their specific HS codes against the FTA schedule and identify which components or engineering products benefit, by how much, and over what timeline. Some imports that were previously unviable may now become commercially workable. However, lower tariffs do not remove India's long-term policy preference for domestic value addition.

Localisation must be planned as a roadmap.

The strongest India strategies do not rely on permanent imports or rushed localisation. They follow a phased model: import where necessary, localise where viable, and move gradually towards higher domestic value addition without compromising quality. A realistic five-year localisation plan is commercially stronger than either full import dependence or premature supplier substitution.

Supplier discipline remains central.

India's supply-chain depth is real, but specialised component gaps remain. EU companies must qualify suppliers carefully, build dual-sourcing for critical parts, and define IP and technology transfer boundaries before production begins. In India, localisation without supplier control creates more risk than benefit.

Logistics resilience is now part of sector planning.

Route disruption and freight volatility have shown that single-route import dependence is fragile. Auto and engineering businesses operating at scale need buffer inventory, alternative shipping pathways, and contract provisions that address logistics shocks.

The practical lesson is clear:

Post-FTA success in India's auto and engineering sector will depend less on tariff reduction alone, and more on how well companies integrate tariffs, localisation, supplier strategy, and logistics resilience into one operating model.

Auto and Engineering Risk-Readiness Checklist (India-Specific)

Supplier Management

☐ Tier-1, Tier-2, and Tier-3 mapping completed

☐ Financial and compliance diligence of key suppliers

☐ Dual-sourcing for critical components

☐ Audit and escalation rights in supplier contracts

☐ Specialised component gaps identified before localisation

Localisation Strategy

☐ Five-year localisation roadmap defined

☐ Component-wise localisation sequencing planned

☐ Local value-addition thresholds monitored

☐ Incentive eligibility aligned with sourcing strategy

☐ Import dependency reduction targets set

Tariff and Pricing Planning

☐ HS classification validated and documented

☐ FTA tariff eligibility mapped product-wise

☐ FTA phase-down timeline built into pricing models

☐ Tariff impact built into sourcing decisions

☐ Customs audit readiness ensured

IP and Technology

☐ Technology transfer boundaries defined

☐ IP ownership and usage controls documented

☐ Supplier NDAs and reverse-engineering restrictions enforced

Logistics Resilience

☐ Buffer inventory policy defined for critical imports

☐ Alternative shipping routes evaluated

☐ Logistics disruption clauses included in supply agreements

What This Chapter Ultimately Means

"In India, competitiveness is not imported. It is built – supplier by supplier, component by component."

India's auto and engineering sector rewards planning, not speed. Supplier fragility, localisation pressure, tariff shifts, and logistics disruption are not exceptions; they are part of the market.

EU companies that treat India as a long-term manufacturing ecosystem are better placed to manage cost, quality and policy risk together.

In this sector, competitiveness is built through supplier control, phased localisation, tariff discipline and operational resilience.

Chapter Takeaway

The common mistake is to view India only through cost or demand. In practice, success depends on whether the business can localise without losing quality, scale without weak supplier dependence, and price correctly while tariffs, freight, and compliance costs keep moving.

Chapter 21

What Should IT, SaaS, and Services Firms Watch For?

Permanent establishment risk, tax characterisation, DPDPA compliance and digital contracts.

For EU IT, SaaS, and services companies, India often looks deceptively simple. No factories, no land, no inventory. Teams can work remotely. Services can be delivered digitally. This creates a dangerous assumption: *"Our India exposure is light."*

In reality, service businesses face some of the most complex regulatory and tax risks in India, especially around permanent establishment, withholding taxes, and contract characterisation. Many foreign services firms discover these risks only after revenues scale, audits begin, or tax authorities raise questions retrospectively.

"In India, service risk is invisible until it is expensive."

This chapter explains where IT, SaaS, and services firms most often get caught, and how to structure operations so India remains a growth engine, not a tax dispute.

1. Permanent Establishment (PE): The Single Biggest Risk

The Reality

Permanent Establishment risk arises when Indian tax authorities conclude that a foreign company has a sufficient business presence in India to justify taxing its profits locally. For IT and SaaS firms, PE risk often arises without any intention to create it.

Triggers commonly include:

- employees or founders operating from India
- Indian teams negotiating or concluding contracts
- long-term client-facing activity from India
- dependent agents or captive service entities

Unlike manufacturing PE, services PE is fact-driven, not asset-driven.

Real-World Pattern (Seen Repeatedly in Practice)

EU SaaS companies often allow senior sales, product, or delivery leaders to operate from India for "cost efficiency." Over time, these individuals begin negotiating pricing, closing deals, or managing key accounts.

Result: Indian authorities argue that core revenue-generating activity is happening in India → PE exposure → retrospective tax demands.

Lesson: Where value is created matters more than where servers or invoices sit.

"Permanent establishments are created by people, not offices."

2. Taxation of Services and SaaS: Characterisation is Everything

The Reality

India taxes cross-border services based on how income is characterised, not how companies describe it internally. Payments may be treated as:

- business income
- fees for technical services
- royalties (especially for SaaS / software access)

Each category has different tax consequences, including withholding tax obligations.

EU companies often assume that SaaS subscription revenue is straightforward "business income." Indian tax authorities may view the same revenue as royalty or technical services, depending on:

- access to software
- control or usage rights
- customisation
- support and implementation components

3. Withholding Tax: Where Cash Flow Gets Hit

Indian customers are often legally required to withhold tax on payments to foreign service providers. Disputes commonly arise when:

- customers withhold tax conservatively
- treaty benefits are unclear
- characterisation is disputed

This affects cash flow immediately, not theoretically.

Well-structured contracts and tax positions can:

- reduce withholding
- clarify gross-up obligations
- avoid disputes with customers

4. India Delivery Models: Captive, Outsourced, or Hybrid

EU services firms use different India models:

- captive delivery centres
- third-party service providers
- hybrid models

Each has different PE and tax implications.

Common mistakes include:

- captive entities performing revenue-generating functions
- lack of arm's-length pricing documentation
- blurred lines between parent and Indian entity roles

Tax authorities examine **functional reality**, not corporate structure.

"If your India team looks like the business, it may be taxed like the business."

5. Contracting Risk: Services Contracts Are Scrutinised Heavily

Services contracts in India are frequently audited and litigated. Key risk areas include:

- vague scope definitions
- bundled pricing (software + services)
- unclear IP ownership
- open-ended indemnities
- absence of tax allocation clauses

For SaaS companies, contracts must clearly distinguish between:

- licence / access rights
- services
- support
- data processing

Poor drafting increases both tax risk and PE risk.

6. Data, Hosting, and Regulatory Overlay

IT and SaaS firms must also consider:

- data localisation expectations

- sector-specific regulations
- client-driven compliance requirements

While India does not mandate blanket data localisation for all sectors, regulatory expectations are tightening, especially for:

- financial services
- health data
- government contracts

The Positive Reality for IT, SaaS and Services Firms

India remains one of the best global hubs for:

- technology talent
- delivery scale
- cost efficiency

Courts and tax authorities are not hostile to foreign service businesses. They are detail-oriented. Companies that:

- define roles clearly
- document transfer pricing properly
- structure contracts carefully
- monitor PE triggers

operate successfully for decades without major disputes.

IT, SaaS and Services Risk-Readiness Checklist

Permanent Establishment

☐ No India-based personnel concluding or negotiating contracts

☐ Clear role separation between EU entity and the India team

☐ Agency and authority limits documented

Tax and Withholding

☐ Income characterisation analysed (business income vs royalty vs FTS)

☐ Treaty benefits evaluated and documented

☐ Withholding tax positions agreed with customers

India Delivery Model

☐ Captive entity functions clearly defined

☐ Arm's-length pricing documented

☐ No revenue ownership at the India entity level unless intended

Contracting

☐ Clear scope and deliverables

☐ IP ownership and usage rights defined

☐ Tax allocation and gross-up clauses included

☐ PE-safe wording used

Data and Compliance

☐ Data handling and hosting reviewed

☐ Sector-specific regulations mapped

☐ Client compliance obligations assessed

Closing Perspective

India is not a low-risk market for IT, SaaS, and services firms, but it is a manageable one. The biggest dangers are not regulatory hostility or policy shocks.

They are structural oversights: unclear roles, loose contracts, and unmanaged PE exposure.

"In India, services do not remain borderless. They become taxable where value is created."

EU companies that treat India as “just a delivery centre” often face tax surprises. Those that treat it as a strategic jurisdiction requiring deliberate structuring, build scalable, compliant, and profitable operations.

SECTION VIII

WHAT IF THINGS GO WRONG?

This section deals with the point at which commercial planning is tested under pressure. Even well-structured India entries can face disputes, breakdown in partner relationships, regulatory friction, or the need for an orderly exit or restructuring. This section explains how disputes are actually resolved in India, why enforcement strategy must be considered before the contract is signed, and how exits should be designed before the investment becomes difficult to unwind. The central theme is practical: when things go wrong in India, speed, structure, and documentation matter more than broad legal rights. Businesses that prepare for dispute and exit early usually protect value far better than those that react late.

Chapter 22

How Are Disputes Resolved in India?

Litigation vs arbitration: speed, cost, enforceability, and pre-transactional strategy.

For EU companies doing business in India, dispute resolution is not a legal afterthought. It is a business continuity issue. When a dispute hits—non-payment, termination, IP misuse, quality claims, delay, or partner conflict—the question is not, "Who is right?" The question is: How fast can we secure relief, protect assets, and reach a final outcome that can actually be enforced?

> ***"In India, the best dispute strategy is the one that protects value early, not the one that argues best later."***

India offers two primary routes: litigation (courts/tribunals) and arbitration. Both work. Both have strengths. The right choice depends on the dispute type, the counterparty, and what you want to achieve (money recovery, injunction, continuity, exit, or deterrence).

1) Litigation in India: Where it Fits Best

Litigation means resolving disputes through:

- Civil courts / Commercial Courts (contract, recovery, injunctions, IP, etc.)
- Special tribunals (National Company Law Tribunal for company matters, Consumer Disputes Redressal Commissions for consumer matters, Income Tax Appellate Tribunal for tax matters, Labour Courts and Industrial Tribunals for labour matters, and National Green Tribunal for environmental matters)

Where litigation works well

- When you need statutory remedies (certain regulatory and tribunal-only matters)
- When the counterparty has clear assets in India and you want executable court orders
- When you need public precedent or strong deterrence (sometimes in IP)
- When arbitration is not available (no clause, or clause is invalid)

The hard truth

Litigation can be slower and procedural. If the other side decides to delay, courts have tools to control it, but delays still happen. That said, Commercial Courts have improved discipline in many cities and can be effective when your pleadings and documents are clean.

2) Arbitration in India: Why Businesses Prefer It

Arbitration is private dispute resolution based on contract. You pick:

- the seat
- rules
- tribunal composition
- process timetable

Where arbitration works best

> ***"Courts decide rights. Arbitration decides outcomes faster, if you set it up correctly."***

- Cross-border disputes (EU party vs India party)
- High-value contracts (engineering, supply, tech, distribution, JV)
- Situations where confidentiality matters
- Where you want a final decision with limited scope for "endless appeal on merits"

Arbitration is usually faster than full litigation for complex commercial disputes, if the clause is well drafted and the tribunal is disciplined.

3) Time and Cost: A Practical View

Litigation

- Interim relief: can be quick (days to weeks) in urgent cases
- Final outcome: can take longer, especially if evidence is heavy and the other side delays
- Cost: court fees are usually lower, but legal costs can rise due to duration

Arbitration

- **Interim relief:** through tribunal (and sometimes courts)
- **Final outcome:** often faster for commercial disputes with focused procedure
- **Cost:** tribunal + institution fees add cost upfront, but shorter timelines can reduce total spend

Reality check:

The 'cheapest' route is rarely the best route.

The best route is the one that reduces business damage and improves recovery probability.

4) Comparative Analysis: Litigation vs Arbitration

Factor	Litigation (Courts/ Tribunals)	Arbitration
Best for	Statutory/tribunal matters, public enforcement	Commercial contracts, cross-border disputes
Speed	Interim relief can be quick; final outcome can take time	Often faster if clause + tribunal + process are tight
Confidentiality	Public proceedings (generally)	Private process, better confidentiality
Decision-maker	Judge allocated by system	Parties choose arbitrator(s) with domain expertise
Procedural flexibility	More rigid procedure	More control on timelines, evidence, hearings
Cost structure	Lower "entry" cost; higher cost over time	Higher upfront fees; may reduce total time cost
Appeal scope	Wider appeal layers depending on forum	Limited court interference; narrower challenge grounds
Enforcement	Decree/Order enforceable in India	Award enforceable like a decree; foreign awards enforceable under treaty framework
Interim relief	Strong and immediate in many cases	Available; effectiveness improves with good drafting
Relationship impact	Often escalatory / public	Can be more business-like, but still adversarial
Cross-border practicality	Can be complex	Generally preferred for cross-border enforceability

5) Realistic Market-Style Examples

Case Study 1: Distributor non-payment (Litigation first, arbitration second)

An EU consumer goods exporter faced chronic non-payment by an Indian distributor. The contract had arbitration, but the immediate risk was that inventory and receivables would be moved. The company approached the court for urgent interim protection and simultaneously invoked arbitration for the final decision.

> ***"Choose litigation or arbitration based on enforcement and leverage, not based on habit."***

Outcome: Assets were secured early; final award followed later; recovery became feasible.

Lesson: In India, combine urgent court protection with arbitration finality when asset flight risk exists.

Case Study 2: Engineering delay dispute (Arbitration-only, faster closure)

An EU engineering supplier faced a dispute over delay penalties and performance acceptance with an Indian industrial customer. The contract had a strong institutional arbitration clause, a tight procedure, and defined acceptance tests.

Outcome: The tribunal narrowed issues, enforced document discipline, and delivered a final award within a business-usable timeframe.

Lesson: For technical contracts, arbitration works best when the contract defines acceptance criteria and evidence rules.

Case Study 3: Minority investor deadlock (Tribunal route is unavoidable)

An EU minority investor in an Indian JV faced alleged related-party leakage and board deadlock. Even though the SHA had arbitration, certain reliefs (company oppression/mismanagement-style remedies) required a specialised tribunal route.

Outcome: Tribunal-led relief created governance corrections; arbitration handled damages later.

Lesson: Some disputes are forum-driven by law. A good strategy uses the right forum for the right remedy.

6) Strategy: How EU Companies Should Decide

Use arbitration when

- dispute is contractual and high value
- cross-border enforceability matters
- you need confidentiality
- you want limited appeal and a final outcome

Use litigation/tribunals when

- the remedy is statutory (company law, certain regulatory areas)
- you need urgent public injunctions that fit court processes
- there is no arbitration clause or it is defective
- you need precedent or strong public deterrence

The winning approach in India

Most sophisticated companies do not choose "either-or." They structure:

- strong arbitration for final resolution and
- fast interim relief tools for early leverage and asset protection.

India's dispute resolution system is not anti-business. It is procedural, evidence-driven and increasingly commercial in approach, especially in arbitration and commercial courts. EU companies that draft dispute clauses carefully, maintain clean documentation during performance and act early when disputes begin usually do well.

The real risk is not choosing the "wrong" forum. The real risk is choosing late, after leverage is lost.

In cross-border disputes between European and Indian parties, the cases that resolve fastest and at the lowest cost share one characteristic: the dispute clause was drafted with precision before the relationship began, and interim relief options were understood before they were needed.

Dispute strategy is pre-transactional work, not post-dispute improvisation.

The arbitration clause that specifies institution, seat, rules, and language; the contract provisions that preserve interim court applications alongside arbitration; and the evidence management practices that start from day one of performance— these are the investments that determine how quickly and cleanly a dispute resolves when it arrives.

Choosing the Right Dispute Mechanism

For EU companies, the choice between litigation and arbitration in India is not only a legal decision. It is a commercial one. The real questions are: how quickly a resolution is needed, what level of cost is proportionate to the dispute, whether the outcome can be enforced against assets in India, and whether business operations must continue while the dispute is ongoing.

Arbitration usually works better for high-value commercial disputes.

Its main advantages are speed, finality, confidentiality and enforceability. A well-drafted arbitration clause, supported by a recognised seat and institutional rules, generally produces a more commercially useful outcome than foreign court litigation followed by separate enforcement steps in India. For disputes involving distribution rights, supply continuity, IP or other time-sensitive business assets, this difference is often decisive.

Litigation remains relevant, but it must be chosen consciously.

India's commercial courts have improved, especially in key cities, but timelines are still longer than arbitration in most significant contract disputes. For lower-value matters, however, court proceedings may still be proportionate, where institutional arbitration costs would outweigh the claim itself.

Business continuity must be built into dispute planning.

This is where many EU companies get caught. Interim injunctions, termination challenges, and asset-risk situations can disrupt Indian operations long before the final outcome is reached. Contracts should therefore preserve interim relief rights, define what happens during a dispute, and reduce the chance that one party can use proceedings to freeze the other's commercial position.

Dispute Risk Has Become More Operational

Recent trade disruption has made dispute planning even more important. Route closures, freight volatility, sanctions exposure, and supply-chain stress have created a new category of EU–India disputes: delays, non-performance, and compliance-triggered terminations caused not by unwillingness, but by disruption.

These disputes are avoidable only if force majeure, sanctions compliance, notice obligations, and termination rights are drafted clearly from the beginning.

What This Chapter Ultimately Means

In India, dispute mechanism is not a boilerplate choice. It affects speed, leverage, enforceability, and business continuity. EU companies that choose forum, interim relief strategy, and contractual risk allocation carefully are far better placed when pressure arises.

The practical lesson is simple: disputes in India should be planned for before the relationship becomes difficult. The businesses that protect value best are not those that react fastest after a dispute starts. They are the ones that built enforcement, continuity and exit options into the contract from the beginning.

Chapter Takeaway

The common mistake is to treat dispute resolution as a legal back-end issue. In India, it is part of transaction design. Forum choice, enforcement route, interim relief, language, and disruption-related clauses all shape the commercial outcome long before the first notice is sent.

In India, the right dispute mechanism does not merely resolve conflict. It protects the business while the conflict is being resolved.

Chapter 23

How Can We Exit or Restructure Our India Investment?

Buyouts, Secondary Sales, IPOs, Regulatory Exits, and Why Exit Must Be Designed At Entry.

For EU investors, entering India is usually planned with care. Exiting India often is not. That is a mistake. In India, entry creates the opportunity. Exit tests whether the investment was structured properly from the beginning.

This chapter explains the main exit routes that work in India in practice: buyouts, where one shareholder or promoter acquires another's stake; secondary sales, where the stake is sold to a strategic or financial buyer; Initial Public Offerings (IPOs), where the company lists on a stock exchange and investors seek liquidity through the public market; and regulatory exits, where sector rules, approvals, foreign investment conditions, or restructuring requirements shape the path out.

"In India, exits don't fail because they're blocked. They fail because they're poorly prepared."

An IPO is often seen as the most attractive exit because it can deliver valuation uplift, liquidity and visibility. But in India, it is also the most preparation-sensitive route. It depends on years of compliance, governance discipline, clean records and regulatory readiness.

The Four Practical Exit Routes in India

EU investors typically exit or restructure Indian investments through one of four routes:

1. Buyout by promoter or strategic buyer
2. Secondary sale to another investor
3. IPO or listed-market exit
4. Regulatory or forced exit (Distress or Policy-driven)

Each route has a different risk, timeline and value profile.

1. Buyouts: The Most Common and Predictable Exit

A buyout involves selling your stake to:

- the Indian promoter
- a strategic buyer
- a financial sponsor

Why Buyouts Work in India

- faster execution
- negotiated pricing
- fewer public market variables

Real Success Story 1: Holcim's Exit from India

Holcim exited India by selling its cement business to the Adani Group. The exit was structured as a strategic buyout, with clean approvals and tax planning.

Outcome:

- full exit
- strong valuation
- smooth regulatory clearance

Lesson:

Strategic buyouts work best when assets are well-run and governance is clean.

Pros and Cons – Buyouts

"In India, the cleanest exits are usually private, not public."

Pros

- quicker timelines
- negotiated certainty
- lower market risk

Cons

- valuation depends on buyer appetite
- limited competitive tension without multiple bidders

2. Secondary Sales: Passing the Baton

Secondary sales involve selling your stake to another party.

- private equity fund
- strategic investor
- global investor entering India

When Secondary Sales Work

- The business is growing, but it needs a new sponsor
- The promoter wants continuity
- Governance and compliance are strong

Real Success Story 2: AXA's Exit from Bharti AXA

AXA exited its Indian insurance JV by selling to ICICI Lombard. The deal allowed AXA to exit, while the business continued under a stronger domestic platform.

Outcome:

- value preservation
- regulatory approval
- minimal disruption

Lesson: Secondary exits succeed when alignment exists between incoming investor and regulator expectations.

Pros and Cons – Secondary Sales

Pros

- flexibility
- avoids promoter deadlock
- preserves enterprise value

Cons

- buyer diligence can be extensive
- pricing may reflect control discounts

3. IPOs: High Visibility, High Discipline

IPOs are attractive but demanding. They require:

- scale
- compliance maturity
- predictable earnings
- market timing

When IPOs Work

- consumer, tech, or scalable platform businesses
- strong growth narrative
- clean cap table and disclosures

Real Success Story 3: Foreign Investor Exits via Zomato IPO

Several foreign investors partially or fully exited Zomato through its IPO and subsequent market sales.

Outcome:

- liquidity
- valuation uplift (for early entrants)
- staged exits

Lesson: IPOs reward patience and governance, but are not quick exits.

Pros and Cons – IPOs

"An IPO in India is not an exit, it is a transition to a new kind of scrutiny."

Pros

- liquidity
- market-driven valuation
- brand enhancement

Cons

- long preparation time
- market volatility
- post-listing lock-ins and scrutiny

4. Regulatory or Forced Exits: The Hard Way Out

Sometimes exits are not strategic; they are forced by:

- regulatory conflict
- policy change
- prolonged disputes
- unsustainable economics

These exits often destroy value.

Disaster Case 1: Nokia India

Nokia's India position became trapped in a major tax dispute at the same time it was seeking to transfer assets as part of the Microsoft transaction. Asset freezes and litigation turned what should have been a strategic exit into a constrained and uncertain process.

Outcome:

- asset freeze and transfer disruption
- prolonged tax litigation
- weakened exit flexibility

Lesson: Regulatory or tax exposure can directly interfere with transaction execution and destroy exit value.

Disaster Case 2: Cairn Energy

Cairn's India experience showed the longer and more public version of a forced exit. A retrospective tax dispute led to years of arbitration, enforcement efforts, frozen value, and reputational and diplomatic escalation.

"In India, forced exits cost more than failed entries."

Outcome:

- prolonged legal battle
- frozen capital
- public and costly enforcement process

Lesson: Regulatory exits are slow, visible and expensive, even when the investor is ultimately vindicated.

Comparative View: Exit Methods at a Glance

Exit Route	Speed	Value Certainty	Regulatory Risk	Best For
Buyout	High	Medium–High	Medium	Mature assets
Secondary Sale	Medium	Medium	Medium	Growing platforms
IPO	Low	Market-linked	Low–Medium	Scalable brands
Regulatory Exit	Low	Low	High	Distress scenarios

What Actually Makes Exits Work in India

Successful exits across all routes share common features:

- clean shareholding records
- clear exit clauses (puts, calls, tags, drags)
- regulatory compliance history
- tax planning done upfront
- no unresolved promoter disputes

Exits fail when investors assume they can "figure it out later."

Restructuring, Instead of Exiting: A Viable Alternative

Sometimes, the right move is not to exit, but to restructure:

- stake dilution
- management change
- asset carve-out
- debt-equity realignment

India allows flexible restructuring when stakeholders cooperate.

India does not trap capital by design. It rewards investors who **plan exits at entry**, maintain governance, and respect regulatory realities. Buyouts and secondary sales remain the most reliable exits. IPOs deliver scale and liquidity, but demand discipline. Regulatory exits are survivable, but costly.

EU investors who succeed in India treat exit not as a fallback, but as a **designed outcome**.

In India, entry builds opportunity. Exit reveals preparation.

Exit Must Be Designed Before Entry

Exit planning is not a later-stage exercise. In India, it begins at entry. The rights, protections and mechanisms documented on day one usually determine whether an investor exits cleanly or under pressure later.

> ***"An India investment that was not designed for exit has not been fully structured. Entry and exit are the same decision, made in sequence."***

Buyout rights must be drafted early.

Put options, call rights, tag rights, drag rights and transfer restrictions should be built into the shareholders' agreement from the outset. In India, these rights must also work within FDI pricing rules and valuation requirements. An exit formula that looks commercially attractive but is not legally workable creates false protection.

Deadlock routes must be documented, not assumed.

If shareholders reach a serious disagreement, the absence of a clear deadlock mechanism often converts a commercial problem into litigation or prolonged stalemate. Russian roulette, shotgun, sealed-bid, or structured buy-sell mechanisms can work in India when drafted properly. Without them, governance breakdown usually destroys exit value.

Valuation and regulatory change must be planned for.

An exit formula agreed at entry may not remain workable if business value changes materially or regulation shifts. This is especially relevant where sector policy, tax rules, or FTA-driven growth significantly change the economics of the investment. Periodic valuation review and change-of-law protection should, therefore, be considered part of exit design, not later corrections.

Why This Matters in Practice

The most consistent lesson from India exits is simple: successful exits were usually structured early. Failed or value-destructive exits were often the result of rights that were never documented, pricing mechanisms that did not work under Indian law, or governance structures that had no credible route to separation.

In India, the most expensive exit work is often corrective. It involves repairing arrangements that were not built for disagreement, regulatory pressure, or buyer negotiation. The least expensive exit is usually the one whose mechanism was agreed upon before the investment was made.

In India, exit is not a fallback plan. It is part of the original investment structure.

SECTION IX

HOW DO WE PREPARE PROPERLY?

Preparation is not caution. It is the precondition of performance. This section provides the analytical and operational tools that translate everything in the preceding chapters into a structured entry decision. The geopolitical risk chapter supplies a framework for assessing macro, sector, and contract-level exposure. The readiness checklist supplies the board-level questions that must be answered before any India commitment is approved. Together, these chapters reflect a conviction formed through cross-border advisory practice: that the quality of preparation at entry determines the quality of outcomes throughout the India journey. Businesses that enter India with incomplete answers to these questions do not merely face a higher risk. They face avoidable risk, the most expensive kind.

Chapter 24

What Must EU Businesses Do Before the FTA Becomes Fully Operational?

Pre-positioning, contract renegotiation, pricing flexibility, entity restructuring and early partnerships.

The most important commercial window under the India–EU FTA is not only after it becomes fully operational. It is the period before. Businesses that use this window to prepare properly will enter with stronger contracts, better partners, cleaner economics, and fewer avoidable disputes. Those that wait for the FTA to go live before acting will often spend the early opportunity period fixing structure instead of using it.

"The businesses that benefit most from the FTA will often be the ones that prepared before it began."

This chapter focuses on four practical priorities: contract review, pricing flexibility, entity restructuring, and early partnerships.

1. Contract Renegotiation Must Begin Early

EU companies with existing distributor, supply, licensing, or joint venture arrangements in India should treat the FTA as a trigger for contract review. Most of these agreements were negotiated under pre-FTA economics. They usually do not deal properly with:

- tariff reduction
- Rules of Origin risk
- pricing review

- landed-cost changes
- direct versus distributor-led sales models

If contracts are left untouched, tariff benefits often create tension rather than advantage. Indian distributors and counterparties will expect pricing conversations once duties start falling. Businesses that wait for those demands to come usually lose leverage.

What should be reviewed

Contract renegotiation should address:

- how tariff savings are allocated
- who bears origin-compliance cost and risk
- whether exclusivity still makes sense
- whether minimum purchase commitments remain realistic
- whether direct sales rights should now be preserved

These are not minor legal edits. They are part of the commercial framework through which FTA benefit will either be captured or lost.

2. Pricing Flexibility Must Be Built Before It is Needed

The right time to build pricing flexibility is before the tariff schedule starts changing, not after commercial expectations have already formed.

A common mistake is to lock in pricing too early—either through fixed distributor pricing or broad promises about post-FTA savings. That often leaves the exporter exposed if:

- tariff reduction is phased slowly
- origin compliance becomes more expensive than expected
- freight and logistics costs remain high
- the actual landed-cost gain is smaller than assumed

The better approach

Instead of fixed long-term pricing, EU companies should build:

- annual pricing review windows
- tariff-linked repricing triggers
- net landed-cost adjustment mechanisms
- contractual rights to respond to quota, freight, or compliance shifts

Pricing should be based on net economics, not tariff reduction in isolation. A duty benefit is commercially useful only if it survives logistics cost, compliance cost, and partner margin pressure.

3. Entity Structure Should Be Re-Tested Before the Window Opens

Some EU companies entered India earlier through distributors or agents because the economics did not support a subsidiary or direct presence. The FTA may change that.

If lower import duty now makes direct operations commercially viable, businesses should assess that shift before the FTA is fully operational. Moving from a distributor-led model to a subsidiary, branch, or stronger India platform takes time. It may involve:

- new entity formation
- tax and PE review
- regulatory approvals
- re-papering of customer arrangements
- transition or termination of existing distributor relationships

These changes are not immediate. Companies that start restructuring only after the FTA is

"If the economics now support direct presence, the restructuring should begin before the market expects it."

live, often lose the best part of the opportunity window to transition friction.

4. Early Partnerships Will Matter More Than Late Search

The best Indian partners in any sector are rarely available for long once a trade opening becomes commercially visible. Distributors, JV candidates, regulatory advisers, local manufacturers and channel partners are often being approached by multiple foreign businesses at the same time.

That means the pre-FTA period is not only for internal planning, it is also for relationship-building.

Why early partnerships matter

Companies that engage Indian partners early gain:

- better-quality counterparties
- better market intelligence
- clearer pricing feedback
- earlier visibility on competitor activity
- stronger credibility before commercial launch

A company that begins meaningful discussions before the FTA is fully operational is often in a much stronger position than one that begins searching only after the opportunity becomes crowded.

5. Pre-Positioning is a Structured Programme, Not a General Intention

The practical role of advisers in this period is to convert a future trade opening into a present preparation programme.

That usually means:

- reviewing existing contracts for FTA-era adequacy
- re-modelling post-FTA economics

- deciding whether structure should change
- identifying which Indian relationships should be built now
- preparing the compliance and documentation framework needed from day one

This is where early legal and commercial advisory work creates the most value. Counsel engaged before commitments are made usually helps shape the opportunity. Counsel engaged only after problems arise is usually doing damage control at a higher cost.

Common Mistakes EU Businesses Make at This Stage

- waiting for the FTA to become fully operational before reviewing contracts
- assuming tariff reduction alone justifies aggressive price promises
- keeping old distribution structures without re-testing economics
- delaying India entity planning until after the opportunity window opens
- approaching Indian partners too late, after better counterparts are already committed

These mistakes are avoidable.

What This Chapter Ultimately Means

The period before full FTA operation is not a waiting period. It is a positioning period. EU companies that use it well will enter India with stronger contracts, better pricing discipline, more suitable structures, and better partner quality.

Those who wait for certainty before preparing usually enter late and spend the first phase of the opportunity correcting avoidable weaknesses.

"The FTA will reward early preparation more than late enthusiasm."

Chapter Takeaway

The common mistake is to think the FTA becomes commercially relevant only when tariff reduction begins. In practice, the value is captured earlier, when contracts are reworked, pricing flexibility is built, structure is re-tested, and relationships are formed before the market tightens.

Chapter 25

Common Mistakes EU Businesses Will Make—and How to Avoid Them

Rigid structures, weak documentation, compliance assumptions, late entry, and one-time legal advice.

Every FTA creates opportunity. It also creates a predictable set of mistakes.

EU companies entering India under the India–EU FTA will repeat errors that experienced India advisers can usually identify in advance. This chapter sets them out directly, not to be critical, but to make them avoidable. The most expensive India mistakes are rarely dramatic. They are usually small assumptions, weak documents, or delayed decisions that compound over time.

"India does not usually punish businesses for wanting to enter. It punishes them for entering casually."

1. Rigid Distribution Structures That Cannot Adapt

One of the most common mistakes is signing a distributor arrangement that works for year one, but fails by year three.

This usually happens when a company grants:

- wide exclusivity
- long tenure
- weak performance obligations
- no pricing review rights
- limited termination flexibility

When the FTA changes the commercial landscape, those agreements become difficult to fix. A distributor that cannot scale, adapt, or support post-FTA growth often becomes a bottleneck, rather than a channel.

The practical lesson

Distributor structures in India must be built for change, not only for launch. Performance benchmarks, pricing flexibility, territory review, audit rights and clear termination routes should be included from the start.

2. Weak Documentation Across the Supply Chain

Rules of Origin are at the heart of FTA benefits. They are also one of the fastest routes to commercial trouble when documentation is weak.

A business that claims tariff benefit without maintaining:

- supplier declarations
- costing support
- process records
- product traceability
- shipment-matched certificates of origin

is building pricing assumptions on unstable ground.

The commercial damage usually appears later, during an audit, when the original duty saving has already been priced into contracts and customer expectations.

The practical lesson

Documentation is not back-office work. It protects pricing, margin, and customs defensibility. In India, poor documentation often becomes a commercial problem before it becomes a customs problem.

3. Compliance Assumptions Instead of Compliance Planning

This mistake appears in many forms:

- assuming GDPR readiness covers India data law
- assuming EU standards satisfy Indian certification
- assuming customs will "sort itself out"
- assuming the relationship is good enough that contract detail does not matter

These are all versions of the same error: treating India as if it will operate through familiar frameworks, rather than its own.

The cost of this mistake usually appears at the worst time, during a regulatory review, port clearance, tax audit, or dispute.

The practical lesson

Compliance in India must be planned specifically for India. Familiarity with EU systems helps, but it does not replace local legal and regulatory preparation.

4. Entering Too Late

Some EU companies will wait for perfect clarity, final tariff schedules, full regulatory comfort, clearer market proof, or visible competitor success.

By then, the best positions may already be taken.

In India, delay does not only slow growth. It can mean losing:

- stronger distributors
- better partners
- early customer access

- regulatory bandwidth
- channel space
- relationship depth

The practical lesson

India does not require reckless speed, but it does reward prepared early movers. Waiting for complete certainty often means entering after the most valuable opening has narrowed.

5. Underestimating the Localisation Timeline

Many EU businesses assume they can import first and localise much later. In practice, India often compresses that timeline.

This pressure comes from:

- policy incentives
- procurement preference
- customer expectations
- margin logic
- sectoral localisation pressure

A company that planned to localise in year six may find itself forced to move in year three, before supplier development, quality systems, and sourcing strategy are ready.

The practical lesson

Localisation should be treated as part of entry planning, not as a later operational project. A delayed localisation strategy often becomes a rushed and expensive one.

6. Treating Legal Advice as a One-Time Cost

This is one of the most common and most costly mistakes.

Some businesses use legal advisers for entry structuring and then treat legal support as largely complete. That rarely works in India. Tax rules evolve, FDI policy changes, sector regulation shifts, court decisions affect interpretation, and compliance expectations move.

A business that keeps operating on yesterday's legal assumptions eventually discovers the gap through:

- restructuring cost
- tax exposure
- compliance failure
- regulatory friction
- avoidable disputes

The practical lesson

In India, ongoing legal support is not only a protection function, it is a commercial intelligence function. Businesses that understand this usually make fewer corrective detours later.

Common Mistakes EU Businesses Make at This Stage

- locking into inflexible distributor structures
- claiming FTA benefit without documentation discipline
- assuming EU compliance automatically carries into India
- delaying entry until the best positions are gone
- treating localisation as a distant problem
- treating legal advice as an entry-stage formality only

These mistakes are predictable. That is exactly why they are avoidable.

What This Chapter Ultimately Means

"In India, preventable mistakes are often more expensive than external risks."

Most 'India' mistakes are not caused by bad intent or weak products. They are caused by structure that could not adapt, documentation that could not defend the business, and assumptions that were never tested against Indian reality.

The businesses that perform best in India are not always the fastest or the most aggressive. They are usually the ones that enter with flexibility, document properly, plan for localisation, and keep legal and commercial advice working together over time.

Chapter Takeaway

The common mistake is to think that India's success depends mainly on finding the right opportunity. In practice, it depends just as much on avoiding the same predictable errors that weaken otherwise strong market-entry plans.

Are We Truly Ready to Enter India?

A Final Readiness Check From a Lawyer's Perspective

Most EU companies do not struggle in India because the opportunity was misread. They struggle because entry happened before readiness. India does not punish ambition; it punishes informality, assumptions, and half-prepared execution. From a lawyer's perspective, being India-ready does not mean enthusiasm, a local contact, or a signed LOI. It means that risk has been anticipated, documented, and allocated before the business begins.

This chapter is a hard readiness check. It brings together the practical questions a serious India counsel would ask before advising a client to proceed.

The Core Legal Reality

India is not a market that forgives ambiguity. Weak contracts, casual compliance, undefined roles, and undocumented assumptions create problems quickly. At the same time, India is highly predictable for businesses that prepare properly. Where structure is deliberate, contracts are enforceable, and compliance is built in early, outcomes tend to follow a clear path.

> ***"Predictability in India is earned, not assumed."***

The Consolidated India Entry Readiness Checklist

If several items below remain unchecked, entry should be paused, not accelerated.

A. Entity and Structure

☐ Entry model chosen

☐ Shareholding and control structure finalised

☐ Board composition and reserved matters defined

☐ Exit routes built into entry documents

B. Regulatory and Licensing

☐ Product / service regulatory mapping completed

☐ Central and state approvals identified

☐ Timelines built into the go-to-market plan

☐ No assumption of EU approval equivalence

C. Tax and PE

☐ Permanent establishment risk assessed

☐ Withholding tax exposure mapped

☐ Transfer pricing model documented

☐ Expatriate tax reviewed

D. Contracts and Enforcement

☐ India-adapted contracts prepared

☐ Arbitration clause tested

☐ Pricing, termination, and exit clauses stress-tested

☐ Partner / distributor risks contractually controlled

E. People and Employment

☐ Hiring model finalised

☐ Employment contracts India-compliant

☐ Termination and severance risks understood

☐ Secondment / visa structure compliant

F. IP and Brand

☐ Trademarks filed in India

☐ IP ownership protected in contracts

☐ Employee / distributor safeguards in place

☐ Enforcement route identified

G. Compliance and Governance

☐ Compliance calendar created

☐ Audit and reporting systems defined

☐ Local teams trained

☐ Crisis escalation path defined

H. Exit and Restructuring

☐ Buyout / secondary / IPO routes identified

☐ Put, call, tag, and drag clauses included

☐ Regulatory exit risks reviewed

☐ No "exit later" assumption

Where Readiness Usually Fails

Different sectors fail in different places.

Manufacturing and industrial businesses usually fail early – land, zoning, environmental approvals, factory permissions, and localisation planning. These are front-end risks, not later corrections.

Pharma and medical businesses fail when pricing control, product classification, and post-market compliance are underestimated. In India, healthcare growth attracts scrutiny.

Auto and engineering businesses fail when localisation, tariff planning and supplier control are treated separately, instead of together.

IT, SaaS and services firms fail quietly, through PE exposure, contract characterisation and authority creep inside local teams.

Consumer and retail brands fail when trademark timing, distributor control and pricing discipline are weak. In India, brand misuse and channel conflict escalate quickly.

The Lawyer's Final Go / No-Go Questions

Before advising a client to enter India, a serious lawyer asks:

- If this relationship breaks down, are we protected on paper?
- If a regulator intervenes, do we have compliance evidence?
- If a tax authority audits us, is our structure defensible?
- If a partner turns hostile, can we exit?
- If success comes faster than expected, can our framework scale?

If the answer to several of these is "not yet," the right advice is to pause and fix, not proceed.

Board-Level Readiness

Before any board approves India entry, it should be satisfied on 10 points:

1. structure
2. tax
3. compliance
4. customs and origin
5. contracts
6. dispute planning

7. logistics
8. sanctions
9. geopolitical exposure
10. exit design

These are not administrative points; they are the legal and commercial foundations of a workable India strategy.

What This Chapter Ultimately Means

India is not a high-risk market. It is a high-discipline market. Businesses that enter with structured contracts, regulatory humility, tax clarity, and governance foresight usually avoid existential problems. Those that enter quickly but without readiness often spend years correcting what could have been fixed in weeks.

> ***The most expensive words in India are not "compliance required." They are "we assumed."***

This chapter is the final test of that readiness.

The businesses that succeed in India are rarely the fastest.

They are the ones who prepared properly before they began.

PRACTICAL TOOLS

For EU Businesses, Advisers and Consultants

This section brings together the practical tools that convert strategy into execution. Across the earlier chapters, the book explains the legal, commercial, regulatory, and contractual decisions that EU businesses must make before entering India or expanding there under the India–EU FTA.

These tools are provided to help readers apply that analysis in a structured way. They are meant to be working documents, not background reading, useful for board discussions, internal planning, deal preparation, contract review, customs readiness, and adviser coordination.

The objective is simple: to give businesses, lawyers, consultants, and cross-border teams a set of practical reference tools they can return to when moving from interest in India to actual implementation.

1: India Entry Legal Checklist For EU Companies

I. Strategic and Board-Level Readiness

1. Define the primary objective of entering India (export growth, manufacturing, services delivery, R&D, sourcing, investment).
2. Identify whether India entry is short-term market testing or long-term strategic presence.
3. Map how the India–EU FTA is expected to benefit the business (tariffs, services access, IP protection).
4. Conduct a sector sensitivity analysis (strategic / regulated / neutral).
5. Identify geopolitical considerations impacting the sector.
6. Obtain board-level alignment on risk appetite for India.
7. Assign a single internal owner for the India strategy.
8. Approve a phased entry plan rather than a single-step expansion.
9. Decide on acceptable capital exposure limits for the initial phase.
10. Document "go / no-go" triggers.

II. Entry Structure and Legal Form

11. Evaluate entry options: wholly owned subsidiary, JV, branch, liaison office, distributor, franchise, service model.
12. Compare control, compliance, tax and exit implications of each structure.

13. Confirm FDI permissibility for the sector.
14. Check sectoral caps on foreign investment.
15. Identify automatic route vs government approval route.
16. Assess beneficial ownership and ultimate control requirements.
17. Structure shareholding to preserve board control and veto rights.
18. Plan for future dilution, buyouts or secondary sales at entry stage.
19. Evaluate the need for Indian promoters or strategic partners.
20. Document exit feasibility for each structure.

III. Corporate and Governance Setup

21. Reserve company name and incorporate entity in India.
22. Draft Memorandum and Articles of Association aligned with business intent.
23. Put in place a Shareholders' Agreement (if applicable).
24. Define reserved matters requiring investor approval.
25. Structure, board composition, and quorum rights.
26. Appoint resident director(s) as required by Indian law.
27. Register with the Ministry of Corporate Affairs (MCA).
28. Set up statutory registers and corporate records.
29. Plan ongoing corporate filings and compliance calendar.
30. Align Indian governance with EU group governance standards.

IV. Tax and Permanent Establishment (PE) Risk

31. Analyse risk of creating **Permanent Establishment** in India.
32. Review activities of Indian employees, agents and distributors.
33. Structure contracts to manage PE exposure.
34. Determine applicable tax residency under DTAA.

35. Obtain Tax Residency Certificate (TRC), if required.
36. Identify withholding tax obligations on payments.
37. Plan transfer pricing model for inter-company transactions.
38. Prepare transfer pricing documentation in advance.
39. Evaluate Place of Effective Management (POEM) risk.
40. Register for PAN, TAN, and GST (if applicable).
41. Align GST classification with customs classification.
42. Plan, repatriation of profits, and dividend taxation.
43. Assess indirect tax implications on imports and services.
44. Model tax costs under best-case and audit scenarios.
45. Put tax audit and dispute management strategy in place.

V. Trade, Customs and FTA Readiness

46. Identify correct HS codes for all products.
47. Confirm eligibility under India–EU FTA.
48. Analyse tariff staging and quotas.
49. Map Rules of Origin requirements.
50. Validate sourcing and manufacturing processes for ROO compliance.
51. Align ROO costing with transfer pricing.
52. Establish origin documentation and certification process.
53. Train logistics teams on FTA claims.
54. Prepare for customs audits and post-clearance scrutiny.
55. Build fallback pricing if FTA benefit is denied.

VI. Regulatory and Licensing

56. Identify sector regulators (BIS, CDSCO, FSSAI, RBI, etc.).
57. Confirm mandatory licences and registrations.

58. . Sequence approvals to avoid operational delays.
59. Apply for product certifications before shipment.
60. Check state-level approvals for manufacturing or offices.
61. Identify ongoing reporting and renewal obligations.
62. Build regulatory compliance tracker.
63. Plan regulator engagement strategy.
64. Assess exposure to pricing controls (if applicable).
65. Prepare for inspections and audits.

VII. Contracts and Commercial Documentation

66. Draft India-specific contracts (do not reuse EU templates).
67. Define governing law and dispute resolution carefully.
68. Choose a seat of arbitration strategically.
69. Build enforceable termination clauses.
70. Define payment terms and currency risks.
71. Include indemnities and limitation of liability.
72. Insert force majeure and change-in-law clauses.
73. Allocate tax and withholding responsibilities.
74. Build audit and information rights.
75. Draft distributor / franchise agreements with tight controls.
76. Define IP ownership and usage rights clearly.
77. Address exclusivity and non-compete carefully.
78. Stress-test contracts for enforcement in India.

VIII. Intellectual Property and Brand Protection

79. File trademarks in India before market launch.
80. Register copyrights, designs or patents, if applicable.

81. Protect trade secrets through contracts and policies.
82. Include IP clauses in employment and vendor agreements.
83. Monitor for infringement and counterfeiting.
84. Set up enforcement and takedown mechanisms.
85. Plan customs recordal for IP protection.

IX. Employment and Expatriates

86. Decide hiring model: employees vs consultants.
87. Draft India-compliant employment contracts.
88. Classify employees correctly under labour laws.
89. Register under applicable labour statutes.
90. Structure compensation, bonuses, and ESOPs.
91. Plan termination and severance costs.
92. Structure secondments carefully.
93. Address visa and immigration requirements.
94. Plan expat tax and social security.
95. Train managers on Indian employment law realities.

X. Data Protection, IT and Cybersecurity

96. Map data flows involving India.
97. Assess compliance with DPDP Act and sectoral data rules.
98. Align GDPR and Indian data requirements.
99. Review cloud hosting arrangements.
100. Ensure data localisation where required.
101. Appoint data protection responsibility.
102. Draft privacy policies and notices.
103. Put incident response and CERT-In reporting in place.

104. Update IT and cybersecurity policies.
105. Train teams on data handling obligations.

XI. Compliance, ESG and Sustainability

106. Establish compliance framework and code of conduct.
107. Implement anti-bribery and anti-corruption controls.
108. Align with Trade and Sustainable Development commitments.
109. Monitor labour, environment, and ESG compliance.
110. Prepare for whistleblower complaints.
111. Maintain audit trails and documentation.
112. Conduct periodic compliance audits.

XII. Dispute Management and Enforcement

113. Prepare dispute escalation protocol.
114. Decide litigation vs arbitration strategy.
115. Identify enforcement routes for awards and judgements.
116. Budget for dispute timelines and costs.
117. Monitor counterparties for insolvency risk.
118. Understand NCLT and insolvency exposure.
119. Preserve evidence and documentation.

XIII. Exit and Restructuring

120. Build exit rights into entry documents.
121. Plan buyout and secondary sale mechanisms.
122. Address FEMA and pricing guidelines for exits.
123. Evaluate IPO feasibility (India or abroad).
124. Plan tax-efficient exit structures.
125. Prepare contingency plans for forced exits.

2: FTA and Rules of Origin Checklist

I. Product and Classification Readiness

1. Confirm correct HS Code at 6, 8 and 10-digit levels (EU + India).
2. Validate HS classification with customs advisers in both jurisdictions.
3. Check whether the product is fully covered, partially covered, or excluded under the FTA.
4. Identify tariff staging period applicable to the product.
5. Verify whether any quota or TRQ (tariff-rate quota) applies.
6. Confirm if the product falls under sensitive or excluded lists.

II. Applicable Rules of Origin (ROO)

7. Identify the specific ROO rule applicable to the product line.
8. Determine whether ROO is based on:
   - wholly obtained, or
   - substantial transformation.
9. Check Change in Tariff Heading (CTH / CTSH / CC) requirements.
10. Verify Regional Value Content (RVC) threshold, if applicable.
11. Confirm allowed tolerance / de minimis percentage.
12. Review product-specific ROO annexes carefully (do not rely on summaries).

III. Supply-Chain Mapping

13. Map origin of all raw materials and components.
14. Identify non-originating materials in the bill of materials (BOM).
15. Check if inputs are sourced from third countries not covered by the FTA.
16. Validate whether processing in the EU or India meets substantial transformation tests.
17. Confirm no simple operations (packing, labelling, minor assembly) are relied upon.
18. Review outsourcing or contract manufacturing arrangements for ROO impact.

IV. Manufacturing and Processing

19. Document manufacturing steps in detail.
20. Maintain records proving value addition at each stage.
21. Ensure manufacturing processes are consistent across shipments.
22. Check that subcontractors follow documented and auditable processes.
23. Confirm, no post-manufacturing processing in non-FTA countries that breaks origin.

V. Costing and Value Calculation

24. Maintain product-wise cost sheets aligned with ROO methodology.
25. Separate originating vs non-originating costs clearly.
26. Align ROO costing with transfer pricing documentation (where applicable).
27. Ensure costing methodology is consistent year on year.

28. Validate currency conversion and valuation rules used in calculations.

VI. Documentation and Certification

29. Identify correct proof of origin mechanism (certificate, self-certification).
30. Ensure origin declaration format matches FTA requirements exactly.
31. Confirm authorised signatory for origin declarations.
32. Maintain supplier declarations for originating inputs.
33. Retain origin records for the mandatory retention period.
34. Ensure ERP/systems capture ROO-relevant data accurately.

VII. Customs and Audit Preparedness

35. Prepare for post-clearance customs audits.
36. Maintain a central ROO audit file for each product.
37. Train logistics and trade teams on ROO claims discipline.
38. Avoid blanket ROO claims without shipment-level verification.
39. Conduct periodic internal ROO reviews.
40. Establish escalation protocol if ROO eligibility changes mid-year.

VIII. Risk Management and Governance

41. Identify financial exposure if ROO claim is denied (duty, interest, penalty).
42. Build contractual protection with suppliers for false origin declarations.
43. Include ROO risk allocation clauses in distributor / customer contracts.
44. Monitor regulatory and interpretational changes under the FTA.
45. Have a response plan for customs queries or investigations.

IX. Strategic and Commercial Alignment

46. Assess whether FTA benefit materially improves pricing competitiveness.
47. Re-evaluate sourcing strategy to optimise ROO compliance.
48. Consider localisation or process changes to strengthen origin status.
49. Align ROO strategy with long-term India / EU market plans.
50. Obtain periodic legal and customs sign-off before major trade expansions.

3: Top 25 Contract Clauses—India Risk Lens

1. Governing Law

This Agreement shall be governed by and construed in accordance with the laws of **[chosen EU jurisdiction or neutral international law]**, excluding conflict-of-law principles that would otherwise refer the matter to another jurisdiction. The Parties acknowledge that this is a cross-border commercial arrangement and that selection of a neutral or EU governing law promotes predictability, commercial balance, and uniform interpretation. Mandatory provisions of Indian law shall apply solely to activities physically performed in India and only to the extent strictly required by statute. The Parties agree that contractual risk allocation, limitation of liability, and commercial structure shall be interpreted consistently with the governing law selected, thereby reducing uncertainty arising from multiple legal systems.

Consequence if ignored:

Default application of Indian law may expand judicial discretion, create interpretational variability across courts, and increase enforcement timelines, potentially exposing EU companies to unpredictable outcomes and higher legal costs.

2. Dispute Resolution and Arbitration

Any dispute, controversy or claim arising out of or relating to this Agreement, including any question regarding its existence, validity, interpretation, performance, breach or termination, shall be finally resolved by arbitration administered by **[ICC – International Chamber of Commerce / SIAC – Singapore International Arbitration Centre / LCIA – London Court of International Arbitration / HKIAC – Hong Kong International Arbitration Centre / DIAC – Dubai International Arbitration Centre / SCC – Arbitration Institute of the Stockholm Chamber of Commerce / VIAC – Vienna International Arbitral Centre / Swiss Arbitration Centre / MCIA – Mumbai Centre for International Arbitration]** in accordance with its applicable rules. The seat of arbitration shall be **[neutral venue]**, and the language of the arbitration shall be English. The Parties acknowledge that arbitration offers confidentiality, procedural neutrality and commercially effective enforcement across jurisdictions. The arbitral tribunal shall have the power to grant interim, conservatory and final relief in accordance with the governing law and the applicable arbitral rules. Recourse to national courts shall be limited to enforcement of the award or urgent interim measures strictly necessary to preserve rights pending constitution of the tribunal or conclusion of the arbitration.

Consequence if ignored:

Poorly drafted arbitration provisions or reliance on local litigation may result in jurisdictional conflicts, extended procedural timelines, and reduced predictability in resolving cross-border disputes involving Indian operations.

3. Jurisdiction Management

The Parties agree that arbitration shall constitute the exclusive forum for dispute resolution, and that parallel proceedings in any national court shall be avoided unless required by law for interim relief or enforcement of awards. Each Party irrevocably waives objections based on forum non conveniens or similar principles that could undermine the agreed dispute framework. The purpose of this clause is to ensure centralised adjudication, minimise duplicative litigation, and preserve commercial certainty in cross-border transactions. The Parties further agree to cooperate in good faith to prevent conflicting proceedings that could delay resolution or increase legal expenditure.

Consequence if ignored:

Parallel litigation in Indian courts alongside arbitration may lead to inconsistent rulings, increased legal expenses and prolonged dispute resolution, weakening enforcement certainty and commercial stability.

4. Scope Definition

The scope of this Agreement is strictly limited to obligations expressly stated herein. No duties shall arise by implication, prior dealings, trade practices, or informal communications unless incorporated through a formally executed written amendment. Deliverables, timelines, technical standards, and performance metrics shall be clearly documented to reflect the Parties' commercial intent. Any additional work requested outside the defined scope shall require a written agreement on revised terms, including pricing and liability allocation. This clause ensures that contractual expectations remain transparent and prevents unintended expansion of responsibilities, particularly in cross-border arrangements where differing business practices and regulatory expectations may otherwise create ambiguity.

Consequence if ignored:

Indian courts may infer broader obligations from conduct or correspondence, potentially extending liability beyond negotiated terms and exposing EU companies to unexpected operational or compliance risks.

5. Independent Relationship

Nothing contained in this Agreement shall be construed as creating a partnership, joint venture, agency, or employment relationship between the Parties. Each Party shall act as an independent contractor, responsible for its own personnel, regulatory compliance, and operational decisions. The counterparty shall not represent itself as having authority to bind the EU company, except where expressly authorised in writing. The Parties acknowledge that maintaining clear independence is essential to avoid unintended tax exposure, employment liabilities, or regulatory obligations arising from local activities. This clause reflects the intention to preserve commercial autonomy while allowing cooperation within clearly defined contractual parameters.

Consequence if ignored:

Mischaracterisation of the relationship may lead to vicarious liability, labour law exposure or tax risks for EU companies arising from actions taken independently by local partners or representatives.

6. Authority Limitations

The counterparty shall not make representations, warranties, or commitments on behalf of the EU company without prior written authorisation. Any statement or undertaking made outside agreed authority shall not bind the EU company unless expressly ratified in writing. Internal communication protocols shall be established to ensure that customer negotiations, regulatory interactions, and commercial commitments remain within defined limits. This clause safeguards against unintended obligations that may arise from enthusiastic local negotiations or differing business practices. The Parties recognise that clarity of authority is essential in cross-border transactions where cultural expectations regarding representation and decision-making may vary significantly.

Consequence if ignored:

Local representatives may unintentionally create contractual or tax obligations, exposing EU companies to third-party claims, compliance challenges, or reputational risks arising from unauthorised commitments.

7. Tax Presence Safeguard

The Parties acknowledge that activities under this Agreement are structured to avoid the creation of a Permanent Establishment or taxable presence for the EU company in India, unless expressly agreed. The counterparty shall conduct negotiations, contract conclusions, and customer interactions within clearly defined limits designed to preserve this structure. Any deviation or regulatory concern shall be promptly disclosed to allow corrective action. The Parties shall cooperate in maintaining documentation demonstrating independent operations and appropriate allocation of functions, assets, and risks. This clause reflects the importance of managing cross-border tax exposure in a manner consistent with international tax treaties and evolving Indian enforcement practices.

Consequence if ignored:

Unintended Permanent Establishment exposure may trigger tax audits, retrospective assessments, interest and penalties, significantly affecting profitability and creating prolonged compliance challenges.

8. Payment Mechanics

All payments shall be made in the agreed foreign currency through authorised banking channels compliant with applicable foreign exchange regulations. Invoices shall specify applicable taxes, currency conversion methodology, and payment timelines to minimise ambiguity. The Parties shall ensure that payment processes support transparent financial reporting and cross-border remittance requirements. Any delay in payment shall attract agreed commercial remedies without suspending performance unless expressly permitted. This clause promotes financial clarity and reduces risks associated with currency fluctuations, banking compliance, or regulatory restrictions affecting repatriation of funds from India.

Consequence if ignored:

Unclear payment structures may lead to foreign exchange complications, delayed remittances, and disputes over tax treatment, affecting cash flow and increasing administrative burdens for EU companies.

9. Withholding Adjustment

Where withholding taxes are imposed under Indian law, the Parties shall cooperate to obtain treaty benefits, certificates, or documentation necessary to minimise withholding, consistent with applicable tax treaties. Payment structures shall reflect the commercial intent agreed between the Parties, ensuring that taxation does not distort negotiated pricing. The counterparty shall assist in securing necessary filings or confirmations required to claim reduced rates where available. This clause recognises that cross-border payments often involve complex tax considerations and therefore encourages proactive cooperation to avoid avoidable financial leakage or disputes arising from differing interpretations of tax obligations.

Consequence if ignored:

Excess withholding may reduce expected revenue, create administrative disputes, and complicate recovery of taxes through refunds or treaty claims, affecting overall commercial viability.

10. Regulatory Compliance

Each Party shall comply with all laws and regulations applicable to its activities under this Agreement. The counterparty shall be responsible for obtaining and maintaining licences, registrations, certifications, and approvals required under Indian law, ensuring that EU companies are not indirectly exposed to local regulatory breaches. The Parties shall cooperate in sharing information necessary to demonstrate compliance during audits or inspections. This clause reflects the understanding that regulatory responsibility should align with operational control, particularly where EU companies rely on local partners for execution within India's regulatory framework.

Consequence if ignored:

Regulatory failures by local partners may lead to investigations, operational interruptions, and reputational damage, potentially affecting EU companies, despite limited involvement in day-to-day compliance activities.

11. Ethics, Anti-Corruption and Trade Compliance

Each Party shall conduct its activities in accordance with all applicable anti-corruption, anti-bribery, sanctions, export control, and responsible business conduct laws, including those applicable within the European Union and India. The counterparty shall maintain internal policies, training programmes, and monitoring mechanisms reasonably aligned with internationally recognised compliance standards. No payment, gift, facilitation, or advantage shall be offered or accepted in connection with this Agreement in a manner inconsistent with applicable laws or ethical expectations. The EU company shall have the right to request reasonable compliance confirmations where credible concerns arise. Any conduct exposing the EU company to sanctions risk, regulatory investigation, or reputational harm shall constitute a material breach, permitting appropriate contractual remedies, including suspension of performance where commercially justified.

Consequence if ignored:

Failure to address compliance risks may expose EU companies to cross-border investigations, reputational damage or sanctions exposure. Indian enforcement actions can trigger wider EU regulatory scrutiny, disrupting operations and investor confidence.

12. Confidentiality and Information Protection

Each Party shall treat all non-public information received under this Agreement as confidential and shall use such information solely for performance of contractual obligations. Confidential information may be disclosed only to personnel, advisers, or affiliates with a legitimate need to know, subject to equivalent confidentiality obligations. The counterparty shall implement reasonable organisational and technical safeguards to prevent unauthorised access, copying, or disclosure, including restrictions on subcontractors and vendors. Confidentiality obligations shall survive termination for a reasonable period consistent with the nature of the information. The EU company may seek equitable relief where disclosure risks cannot be adequately remedied through monetary damages, acknowledging the importance of preserving commercial strategy, pricing models, and proprietary methodologies within the Indian market context.

Consequence if ignored:

Weak confidentiality protections can lead to loss of competitive advantage, uncontrolled sharing with distributors or competitors, and difficulty obtaining effective injunctive relief in India once confidential information becomes widely circulated.

13. Intellectual Property Ownership and Control

All intellectual property rights existing prior to this Agreement or developed independently shall remain the exclusive property of the originating Party. Any materials, improvements, adaptations, or deliverables created in connection with this Agreement shall be assigned or licensed only as expressly agreed in writing. The counterparty shall not register trademarks, domain names, designs, or similar rights incorporating the EU company's intellectual property without prior written consent. The EU company retains sole discretion over enforcement strategy, licensing decisions, and brand positioning within India. Where local law requires formal documentation for ownership recognition, the counterparty shall cooperate in executing such documentation promptly. The Parties acknowledge that clarity of ownership is essential to avoid disputes over derivative works, technology transfers, or brand usage in rapidly evolving Indian markets.

Consequence if ignored:

Ambiguity around ownership may allow local parties to assert rights over technology or branding, creating long-term disputes, enforcement challenges and restrictions on expansion or restructuring within the Indian market.

14. Intellectual Property Ownership and Control

All intellectual property rights existing prior to this Agreement or developed independently shall remain the exclusive property of the originating Party. Any materials, improvements, adaptations, or deliverables created in connection with this Agreement shall be assigned or licensed only as expressly agreed in writing. The counterparty shall not register trademarks, domain names, designs, or similar rights incorporating the EU company's intellectual property without prior written consent. The EU company retains sole discretion over enforcement strategy, licensing decisions, and brand positioning within India. Where local law requires formal documentation for ownership recognition, the counterparty shall cooperate in executing such documentation promptly. The Parties acknowledge that clarity of ownership is essential to avoid disputes over derivative works, technology transfers, or brand usage in rapidly evolving Indian markets.

Consequence if ignored:

Ambiguity around ownership may allow local parties to assert rights over technology or branding, creating long-term disputes, enforcement challenges and restrictions on expansion or restructuring within the Indian market.

15. Permitted Use of Intellectual Property

The counterparty is granted only a limited, revocable, non-exclusive and non-transferable right to use the EU company's intellectual property solely for purposes expressly authorised under this Agreement. Such use shall comply with brand guidelines, quality standards and applicable regulatory requirements. The counterparty shall not modify, sublicense, reverse engineer or exploit the intellectual property beyond the agreed scope without prior written approval. Any goodwill arising from use of the EU company's intellectual property shall accrue exclusively to the EU company.

Upon termination or expiry, all usage rights shall immediately cease, and the counterparty shall return or destroy all materials bearing the EU company's intellectual property. This structure ensures consistency of brand integrity and technology control across jurisdictions.

Consequence if ignored:

Overbroad IP usage rights may lead to parallel branding, unauthorised sublicensing, or market confusion. Rectifying misuse in India can be costly and time-consuming, particularly where local goodwill has already been created.

16. Data Protection, Cybersecurity and Cross-Border Data Handling

The Parties shall process personal data strictly in accordance with applicable EU data protection standards and Indian data protection laws, including lawful processing principles, purpose limitation, and security obligations. The counterparty shall implement reasonable technical and organisational safeguards, maintain records of processing activities, and notify the EU company promptly of any actual or suspected data breach. Cross-border data transfers shall be undertaken only where lawful mechanisms are in place and where necessary for the performance of this Agreement. The counterparty shall cooperate with audits or regulatory inquiries relating to data handling practices. The EU company may require corrective measures where data processing activities present a material risk to compliance or reputation, ensuring that cross-border digital operations remain legally sustainable.

Consequence if ignored:

Non-compliance with data laws may lead to regulatory investigations, operational restrictions, and reputational harm. In India, enforcement often begins with audits or directives that can significantly disrupt service delivery and client trust.

17. Audit, Inspection and Verification Rights

The EU company shall have the right, upon reasonable prior notice, to conduct audits or request independent verification of compliance with this Agreement, including regulatory obligations, data protection practices, financial records directly relevant to performance, and adherence to agreed operational standards. Such audits shall be conducted during normal business hours and in a manner that minimises disruption to business operations while preserving confidentiality. The counterparty shall maintain accurate and complete records for a reasonable retention period and shall cooperate in good faith with any audit process. Where deficiencies are identified, the counterparty shall implement corrective measures within agreed timelines. The intent of this clause is preventive oversight rather than intrusive control, enabling early identification of compliance gaps that may otherwise escalate into regulatory or commercial disputes within India's evolving enforcement environment.

Consequence if ignored:

Absence of audit rights limits visibility into local operations, allowing compliance failures or financial irregularities to remain undetected until regulatory intervention or disputes arise, increasing reputational and legal exposure.

18. Indemnity and Risk Allocation

Each Party shall indemnify and hold harmless the other from losses, liabilities, claims, penalties, or costs arising from breach of contractual obligations, violation of applicable law, or negligence attributable to its actions or omissions. The counterparty shall bear primary responsibility for matters arising from local regulatory compliance, employment practices, or third-party conduct within India. Indemnification shall include reasonable legal expenses incurred in defending claims. This provision reflects a balanced allocation of operational risk, recognising that the EU company relies on local execution while maintaining appropriate contractual protection against actions beyond its direct control. Indemnity obligations shall survive termination for a reasonable period to address claims that may arise after completion of services or delivery of products.

Consequence if ignored:

Without clear indemnity allocation, EU companies may absorb costs linked to local regulatory breaches or third-party disputes, undermining financial predictability and complicating insurance or risk management strategies.

19. Limitation of Liability and Commercial Balance

Except where prohibited by applicable law, neither Party shall be liable for indirect, incidental, or consequential damages, including loss of profit or business opportunity. The aggregate liability of the EU company under this Agreement shall be proportionate to the commercial value derived from it, reflecting a fair allocation of risk relative to control. Liability caps shall not apply to confidentiality breaches, intellectual property misuse, or compliance violations, to the extent legally permissible. This clause ensures commercial predictability while recognising that cross-border arrangements involve multiple regulatory and operational variables. The Parties acknowledge that limitation of liability provisions support long-term collaboration by aligning exposure with reasonable business expectations rather than open-ended risk.

Consequence if ignored:

Unlimited liability exposure may create disproportionate financial risk for EU companies, particularly where local enforcement practices expand damages or where indirect losses are claimed through extended litigation.

20. Force Majeure and Performance Disruption

Neither Party shall be liable for failure to perform obligations due to events beyond reasonable control, including natural disasters, governmental restrictions, or significant disruptions affecting operations. The affected Party shall provide prompt written notice and undertake reasonable efforts to mitigate impact and resume performance as soon as practicable. Economic hardship, foreseeable regulatory changes, or internal workforce issues shall not automatically qualify as force majeure unless explicitly agreed. This clause seeks to preserve commercial continuity while preventing misuse of force majeure provisions in environments where operational challenges may arise due to regulatory or market conditions. The Parties shall consult in good faith to determine whether temporary suspension or adjustment of obligations is appropriate.

Consequence if ignored:

Overly broad force majeure language may allow avoidable delays or non-performance to be justified, reducing operational certainty and creating disputes regarding responsibility for missed deadlines or contractual obligations.

21. Change in Law and Regulatory Adjustment

If a change in applicable law or regulatory framework materially affects performance, cost structure, or commercial feasibility, the Parties shall engage in good-faith discussions to adapt the Agreement in a manner that preserves its economic balance. Such adjustments may include modification of pricing, timelines, or operational scope. Where continuation becomes impracticable despite reasonable efforts, either Party may consider suspension or structured termination. This clause recognises that regulatory evolution in India can influence market conditions, taxation, or compliance obligations, and therefore establishes a collaborative mechanism for addressing unforeseen legal developments without undermining the overall commercial relationship.

Consequence if ignored:

Absence of a structured change-in-law mechanism may force EU companies to absorb unexpected regulatory costs or continue under commercially unsustainable conditions, increasing pressure to litigate rather than renegotiate.

22. Termination Rights and Business Flexibility

Either Party may terminate this Agreement upon a material breach by the other Party that remains uncured after reasonable written notice. In addition, the EU company may terminate for legitimate business reasons, including restructuring, regulatory risk, or strategic realignment, upon defined notice while honouring accrued obligations. Upon termination, the counterparty shall promptly cease use of intellectual property, return confidential information, and assist in an orderly transition of operations where reasonably requested. Termination shall not affect rights or liabilities accrued prior to termination. The Parties acknowledge that cross-border commercial relationships evolve over time, and therefore, termination provisions should enable responsible exit without creating unnecessary operational disruption or reputational harm within the Indian market.

Consequence if ignored:

Rigid or unclear termination provisions may lock EU companies into underperforming arrangements, making exit legally complex and commercially expensive, particularly where local relationships or regulatory dependencies exist.

23. Non-Solicitation and Relationship Protection

During the term of this Agreement and for a reasonable period thereafter, the counterparty shall refrain from directly or indirectly soliciting key employees, consultants, or customers introduced through this relationship, except with prior written consent. The intent of this clause is to preserve stability of teams, protect investments in market development, and maintain trust between the Parties. Any permitted engagement shall occur only through mutually agreed commercial arrangements. The Parties recognise that the Indian market often involves close collaboration with local personnel and partners; therefore, clear expectations around non-solicitation help avoid misunderstandings and safeguard long-term relationships without imposing unreasonable restrictions on lawful business activities.

Consequence if ignored:

Unrestricted solicitation can lead to the loss of trained personnel or customer relationships, weakening EU companies' market position and undermining investments made in building a local presence and brand credibility.

24. Assignment and Change of Control

The counterparty shall not assign, transfer or subcontract its rights or obligations under this Agreement without the prior written consent of the EU company, which shall not be unreasonably withheld. The EU company may assign this Agreement to an affiliate or successor entity upon written notice, provided that performance obligations remain substantially unchanged. Any change in control affecting the counterparty shall be promptly disclosed to allow assessment of continued suitability and compliance. This clause reflects the importance of transparency and continuity in cross-border arrangements, ensuring that unexpected ownership changes do not introduce unforeseen regulatory, reputational or operational risks for the EU company operating within India.

Consequence if ignored:

Uncontrolled assignment or ownership changes may introduce unknown counterparties or risk profiles, potentially exposing EU companies to compliance concerns, reputational issues, or disruption of established operational standards.

25. Governing Language and Interpretation

This Agreement shall be executed in English, which shall prevail over any translated or local-language versions for purposes of interpretation and enforcement. Where translations are required for regulatory or operational purposes within India, such translations shall be treated as reference documents only and shall not alter the meaning of the original English text. The Parties acknowledge that clarity of language is essential to prevent interpretational disputes in cross-border agreements, particularly where multiple legal systems and business cultures interact. Any ambiguity shall be interpreted in a commercially reasonable manner consistent with the Agreement's stated objectives rather than informal communications or unilateral interpretations.

Consequence if ignored:

Translation inconsistencies may create disputes over contractual intent, delay enforcement proceedings, and increase litigation costs, particularly where local interpretations diverge from the agreed commercial understanding.

4: India–EU FTA—Indicative Tariff Reference Table

This table provides indicative tariff ranges for major EU export categories under the India–EU Free Trade Agreement. Rates shown are illustrative and based on the FTA framework as described in this book. Actual tariff rates depend on the specific HS code classification of each product. EU exporters should obtain HS code-specific tariff schedules and conduct Rules of Origin analysis before making pricing or entry decisions.

EU Export Category	Pre-FTA Rate (Indicative)	Post-FTA Target Rate	Implementation	Key Considerations for EU Exporters
Machinery and Industrial Equipment	7.5–15%	0–2.5%	5–7 years	Strong advantage for German and Italian manufacturers. Covers CNC, industrial automation, processing equipment.
Chemicals and Specialty Chemicals	7.5–10%	0–2.5%	3–5 years	Phased by sub-category. REACH compliance documentation is required for hazardous substances.

EU Export Category	Pre-FTA Rate (Indicative)	Post-FTA Target Rate	Implementation	Key Considerations for EU Exporters
Pharmaceutical Products	10–12%	0–5%	5 years	Subject to CDSCO registration, pricing controls under NPPA apply post-entry. Compulsory licensing framework remains in force.
Automotive—Vehicles	60–100%	15–40%	7–10 years	Significant reduction, but not zero-rated. PLI scheme for domestic manufacturing offers a parallel incentive for local production.
Automotive—Components and Parts	15–35%	5–10%	5–7 years	Greater reduction than finished vehicles. Localisation policy will accelerate, build a five-year localisation roadmap.
Medical Devices	7.5–12%	0–2.5%	3–5 years	BIS and CDSCO certification are required regardless of tariff status. Device classification and pricing controls apply post-scale.
Textiles and Apparel	10–25%	5–12%	5–7 years	Rules of Origin are critical – substantial transformation required. Value-addition thresholds enforced at customs.

EU Export Category	Pre-FTA Rate (Indicative)	Post-FTA Target Rate	Implementation	Key Considerations for EU Exporters
Processed Food and Beverages	30–100%	15–50%	7–10 years	FSSAI registration mandatory. Many categories retain significant protection. Entry costs remain high in sensitive sub-categories.
Aerospace Components	2.5–10%	0%	3 years	Dual-use export controls apply from the EU side. DGCA approval required for aviation-critical parts.
Electronics and Electrical Equipment	0–20%	0–7.5%	3–5 years	BIS certification mandatory for most product categories. PLI scheme provides competing incentives for local manufacturing.
Luxury Goods and Consumer Products	20–150%	10–75%	7–10 years	Meaningful reduction, but significant duties remain on premium categories. Brand protection and first-to-file IP registration critical before market entry.
Agricultural and Natural Products	30–100%	Varies	10+ years	Many sensitive categories are excluded or have long phase-downs. SPS/phytosanitary compliance required. Verify specific HS codes.

Note: All rates are indicative and illustrative for planning purposes only. Pre-FTA rates reflect India's applied Most Favoured Nation (MFN) tariff ranges for the relevant HS chapters. Post-FTA target rates and implementation periods are based on the FTA framework described in this book. Rates vary materially within each category depending on specific HS sub-headings. Businesses must obtain a product-specific tariff schedule from their customs or trade adviser before the first FTA-benefit shipment. Non-tariff barriers, certification requirements, and pricing regulations operate independently of tariff rates and must be assessed separately.

www.ingramcontent.com/pod-product-compliance
Lightning Source LLC
LaVergne TN
LVHW050928210926
848482LV00013B/567
9798904513603